Man
Under Construction

TRANSFORMING FATHERS, HUSBANDS, AND SONS
AS MEN OF GOD WITH PURPOSE

By

JOSEPH HARRIS

Copyright © 2016 JOSEPH HARRIS

All rights reserved.

ISBN: 1936867214
ISBN-13: 978-1-936867-21-9

DEDICATION

This book is inspired and dedicated to my Father in Heaven, my biological father and mother, Joe Arthur Doyle and Gussie Doyle; my brothers, Chris and Craig. Thanks to my sisters, Linda, Jackie, Joann and Mary, who are precious and inspirational in my life. To my wife, LaDonna, thank you! My wife is always there for me. Please understand the significance of a wife helping a man in his manhood and family. Thank God for His design in making a woman for man.

Thank God for my parents introducing me to Jesus Christ. My prayer is that my parents rejoice in Heaven before God's Throne. My father and mother were responsible for my baptism. I thank God that both of them had vision to get their children in relationship with the Lord, Jesus Christ. They knew the importance of relationship. My mother ensured each son and daughter went into the water, fully immersed, baptized in the name of the Father, the Son and the Holy Ghost.

> I believe both of them knew the power of God. I credit them for guiding me in the right direction in life. This helped me to get on the right path and began my journey and service as a Kingdom Servant of Jesus Christ. Thanks be to God who helped me walk away from the dark side of life. I could have been dead and gone if it had not been for the Lord on my side. If it had not been for the Lord in the life of my parents, who knows which direction I would have taken. God led my parents to train me and guide me to Him.

CONTENTS

	Prayer	8
	Purpose	9
1	The Cost of the Cross	10
2	God Created Man	12
3	Man Searching for God	15
4	God formed You	17
5	Meditate on God!	18
6	A Transformed Man	19
7	God's Gifts to Man	21
8	Overcome Your Identity Crisis	23
9	Prayer Breaks Prison Foundations	24
10	Deliverance Out of Bondage	28
11	Jesus Prayed for His Men	30
12	Justified by the Blood	31
13	The Author & Finisher of My Faith	32
14	God Looks at Man's Heart	34
15	God is Looking for Obedience in Man	36
16	God Called You	38

17	Salvation In Jesus Christ Soul Winner	39
18	A Cup for the World	41
19	Man of God, Kick Demons Out!	42
20	Don't Let Your Family Go to Hell	44
21	Get Ready for a Pentecostal Movement	46
22	Under God's Authority	48
23	A Set Mind	50
24	Man Finding Peace In God	52
25	Man Finding Grace In God's Eyes	54
26	The Power of His Word	56
27	A Holy Spirit Filled Man	58
28	A Man of Faith	59
29	I Will Trust God	61
30	He Restores Life	62
31	Jesus is the Word	64
32	A New Man Raised Up in Christ!	66
33	The Resurrection	68
34	God Set You Free from Egypt!	70
35	A Man with a Dream	72
36	Put Your Soul in Jesus's Hands	74

37	Witness of His Power	76
38	Man in Worship to God	78
39	Man Under the Influence of God	79
40	God Ordained it!	80
41	The Cross	81
42	It is Finished	83
43	Curious Creatures	84
44	Worship God!	85
45	Authority to Bind	86
46	Jesus Called You!	88
47	He is Risen	89
48	Let Your Request Be Known	90
49	Man's Love for God	91
50	Tame that Tongue	92
51	Expect Jesus to Return	94
52	God's Goodness	95
53	The Man that Abides in Christ	96
54	Witnesses of Life	98
55	Crucified with Christ	100
56	New Life!	102

57	A Father's Love for Sons	103
58	God-Given Authority to Man	105
59	Walking in Favor	107
60	The Original Man Advanced	108
61	The Covenant Man	110
62	Moses, The Deliverer	112
63	Lord, Bless Me!	113
64	When Dreams Come True	115
65	Job, A Faithful Man of God	117
66	Listening to God's Voice A Man of Grace	119
67	Samson, The Man	120
68	Love is the Greatest	122
69	Seed Sowers	124
70	Dwell with My Father	126
71	About the Author	128

PRAYER

Dear Lord, I pray that these words will draw me near and help add to my life, the goodness of your grace and love. Father, may all the spiritual scales be removed from my life, today, so that I can know you better and see those visions that you have predestined for my life.

Today, I surrender all to your will and your way. And I acknowledge and repent of my sin before you. Father, because you are the only true and wise God. There is no one like you. You are the only one who can set men free from bondage and the sin that so easily entangles each person. Lord, give me understanding in your truth as I encounter these readings.

Help me to rightly divide this word and meditate day and night on your goodness, as I glorify you. Your word is sharper than a two-edged sword and can penetrate the soul and spirit. I pray that your word will go out and not return void. Father, help me not to be ashamed of the gospel. It is through the power of the word of God that salvation and deliverance are given to those that ask. Lord, I need you to make me over. Create in me a clean heart and renew a right Spirit in me. I am a man under God's construction willing to work to advance the Kingdom.

PURPOSE: This book is intended to build men up to be used in God's Kingdom. His Kingdom specifically impacts the lives of people. You get to win souls for God's Kingdom. Men become soul winners, protectors, providers, and doers of the faith.

It is my prayer that after fifty days and during the process of reading this book every man, and at-risk youth will experience a bond and personal relationship with Jesus Christ.

These readings are specifically for men, fathers and sons who need to know the power of God in their lives. God can hold on to you in the worst moments of life. He comforts you as well as transforms you.

God can take hold of our lives and cause us to be in His perfect will. We belong to Him. He moves perfectly in our lives for His glory. Allow the word of God to change your heart. Watch Him help in all kinds of life situations. I hope that this book will help all people to see God as the head of their lives and home. My intent is that you will be renewed in Christ. He alone can perform in our lives amazing and blessed things. In this book, you will learn how Jesus transformed people immediately and continuously all those that call upon His name.

I hope to share the power of His love and encourage you to make it a priority in your lives. This book will challenge you to see with new vision. You will be encouraged in every scripture to live a better life knowing that God has a hold on you and expects for you to seek Him. His love takes you into the presence of His glorious blessings.

CHAPTER 1
THE COST OF THE CROSS

John 19:16-20: Then Pilate turned Jesus over to them to be crucified. So they took Jesus away. Carrying the cross by himself, he went to the place called Place of the Skull (in Hebrew, Golgotha). There they nailed him to the cross. Two others were crucified with him, one on either side, with Jesus between them. And Pilate posted a sign over him that read, "Jesus of Nazareth, the King of the Jews." The place where Jesus was crucified was near the city, and the sign was written in Hebrew, Latin, and Greek, so that many people could read it.

Gang fighting and bullying were huge where I grew up in Louisiana. They remain a problem in society today. It will take real men to help boys develop while mentoring them and encouraging them so that they can be successful. The goal is to make them better men in society for their families and God's purpose.

If you are standing alongside the bully who leads a gang, then you are just as guilty. Stop the bully and gang member in his tracks. Help him turn around in Jesus name! Encourage him to do something constructive in life!

A friend of mine, Charles was approached while in the park by another person I knew. Fred immediately picked a fight, and to his surprise the person he picked the fight with beat him down. He thought he had an easy victory over Charles because he was standing with his gang buddies. Charles surprised him with his strength and level of authority and confidence. The next time he saw Charles he had respect and walked the other way. You see, unfortunately for him he had received a black eye, bloody nose and a bad headache. They messed with the wrong person that day. A similar thing happened but it was a little different and more powerful. Jesus gave the devil a black eye and bloody nose in his defeat.

It can be tough trying to carry your cross because the enemy is constantly seeking to start a fight. Jesus could have viewed us as the enemy but he didn't. One of my favorite scriptures comes from Matthew 16:23-25 which talks about denying yourself. It admonishes us to take up our cross and follow Him. It takes a man who is totally unselfish and not pride centered to follow Jesus. He must be full of confidence, faith, and love; and truly believe in Jesus in order to pick up his cross. Real men avoid strife, violence, and hatred in their hearts. A true man will carry his cross regardless of who is around him. A true man will prove to his family that Jesus is the head of his life, Lord and Savior! Make no mistake about it, people at work and everywhere will notice you as one of Jesus's men! What a blessed identity to have! The man that God creates will find himself under construction. He will go through hell, high waters and back. Look at John 19 at what Jesus did for you and me. He faced Pilate and never denied who He was; nor did He give up His mission to die. The cross he carried was for all of us.

Men, when are you going to carry your cross? Jesus paid it all to redeem us. Yet some men are still in defiance to God as they walk under the blessings of Jesus's death, burial and resurrection. Today, ask God to do a complete transformation inside your heart. Allow the Holy Spirit to do construction in your heart, mind and spirit. Ask Him to pour his spirit inside and sanctify your heart today! Wait for it and expect it! Jesus is Lord!

CHAPTER 2
GOD CREATED MAN

Genesis 1:15 -17 The Lord God placed the man in the Garden of Eden to tend and watch over it. But the Lord God warned him, "You may freely eat the fruit of every tree in the garden except the tree of the knowledge of good and evil. If you eat its fruit, you are sure to die."

God created man and no one else had anything to do with it! When you look at God giving Adam everything on earth, He was intentionally entrusting everything He created to Adam. He also intended that Adam would take care of the garden and all things that were under his authority and dominion. God gave Adam a paradise. Nothing could pluck Adam out of the hands of God because of his authority. Nevertheless, He also gave Adam the power to choose. Exercising one's own free will is a powerful thing. You can make a choice today to accept Jesus as Lord into your heart and walk in obedience.

The most harmful sin that could destroy Adam's position and blessings was the act of disobedience. Adam made the wrong choice by eating from the tree of knowledge of good and evil. Adam and Eve's disobedience to God symbolized their broken relationship and worship with God. They both made a choice to worship the evil one as soon as they rebelled against God. Today people are still being influenced by the devil. However God reclaimed His people back to Himself. When you worship someone, usually you bow down before them. God did not create you to bow before the devil. You were created to bow before God only. Why do I say this? Adam and Eve obeyed the serpent (devil) rather than obeying God. The majority of society does the same thing today because they are blinded. Not only did Adam obey

Satan, Adam obeyed his wife first rather than God by eating the fruit. . As a result, sin entered the world. Sin runs rampant because of this first family.

What is your family like? Adam was given authority to be Eve's covering against all things: enemies, principalities and wickedness. Eve was not to be the head nor put herself in that position. Adam was positioned as the head by God. The husband is positioned by God as leader of the family. He is supposed to cover the wife and shield her from all evil.

Many households suffer with issue of power struggles today. Some wives put themselves in the wrong position. Every wife must position herself properly so she can honor her husband. She must allow the man to plant seed and lead the family. She must be submissive to her own husband! Otherwise the house is out of order. Adam was created with the ability to choose obedience in God's perfection. One choice can either make you or break you. He fell, along with his wife, because of rebellion and disobedience. Anytime a person ignores God and does what he pleases himself, he steps outside of God's covering, authority and misses out on the blessing. At any moment God could eliminate man as though he never existed and raise up a new one in his place! Think about it, he allowed Jesus to die on the cross and be buried in a tomb, and then raised Him up from the dead. He is God and He can do anything, but fail!

In Genesis chapter 2: 22-23, we read that God brought Eve to Adam as his wife and as a gift to him. God had already laid the foundation and everything that Adam needed in the garden. God had made the garden a paradise for Adam. Adam had this paradise to share with his wife. They lived in a perfect environment and atmosphere. Nothing else was better than what God gave them. God gave his best! All Adam needed to do was be obedient. All dominion and authority was given to Adam. He was in essence a child of God. He had power directly from God. He was not God, although most people believe that he was a little "g" god because he was made in the image of God.

CHAPTER 3
MAN SEARCHING FOR GOD!

Job 11:7-9 "Can you search out the deep things of God? Can you find out the limits of the Almighty? They are higher than heaven what can you do? Deeper than Sheol what can you know? Their measure is longer than the earth and broader than the sea".

An unmanned aerial vehicle (drone) has the capability to support military and civilian operations. It is used to recon and conduct search and rescue missions, as well as weather analysis and surveillances. This small remote aircraft has the ability to expose depth. and magnitudes of the enemy's intelligence. This aircraft, like multitudes of others (the stealth fighter, F15 and F16s), can really expose and eliminate the enemy which in turn gives our soldiers the victory. The Holy Spirit is like a drone. He also gives us the victory as well. We are built better and equipped with the Spirit of the Lord inside of us.

Men who are lost need to invite God to come inside their hearts to make them a new creature in Jesus Christ. The Holy Spirit will make you a better man!

The above passage reminds Job of God's power and knowledge, not limited to anyone or anything. God asks Job, Can you search out the deep things of God? He is referring to God's mystery and His power. It also seems that God is reminding Job o who God really is. Job needed to learn more about his God. God was opening his mind to get him back on track. . He was also checking Job and reminding him that he must rely fully on God for answers. God wanted Job to depend on Him. Although Job can search, he can't find the deep things of God, unless God reveals them to him.

Man has internal instincts to search for God's word and revelation. He also has an instinctive code inside of him to search for God. because he needs God.. Every man longs to search for that missing void in his heart. Life will lead you there because the Holy Spirit hears your call for help. In this passage, God asks these questions to spark a desire to draw you into relationship with Him. When you get in it, don't doubt God's power. He wants you to be continuously under construction so that He can guide your life. God is reassuring us, as saints, that there is no limit to His power. Because He created all things, they fall under his authority! God is reminding us that He gives us the knowledge and revelation that he wants us to have.

God wants us to know that when we search for Him and receive him into our hearts, we have no need to worry about the enemy breaking us down. He cannot steal our joy, peace and salvation. God knows the depths of Hell and how to make the enemy flee. First of all, God has already wrapped His love and grace around His children. The enemy desperately wants to kill you and steal all of your joy. God's grace is stronger because his firm grip and mighty power will not let you go! Today, you can easily make up your mind to accept Christ. We all need Jesus in our lives. He is the God who has all power in His hands.

CHAPTER 4
GOD FORMED YOU

JEREMIAH 1:5: "Before I formed thee in the belly I knew thee; and before thou camest forth out of the womb I sanctified thee, and I ordained thee a prophet unto the nations."

Every man needs to know who is responsible for forming him (Genesis 2:1-7). Nevertheless in the book of Jeremiah, God speaks to Jeremiah informing him that He already knew him before he was formed. God sometimes has to remind us that He is the Creator who knows all things. God was reassuring Jeremiah that God was on his side.

No matter what the battle looks like, God has already predestined it for your success. God set you apart for His purpose and He has blessed you! No matter who comes against you and tries to strike fear into your heart, God has already made you victorious. Wherever you place the sole of your feet, God has already given to you, as a man of God. The request today is to ask God to form good thoughts, good things in your heart that you would not sin against Him. It is time for you to give yourself to God.

Repeat this prayer: "Lord, I ask you to construct me with a new mind. In my new construction, give me my true identity. You reminded Jeremiah that you knew him already in his mother's womb. Let these words remind me that you already see me and that you ordained me for your use in ministry! You've set me apart for your glory!"

CHAPTER 5
MEDITATE ON GOD!

Philippians 4:8: Finally, brethren, whatever things are true, whatever things are noble, Whatever things are just, whatever things are pure and whatever things are lovely, Whatever things are of good report, If there is any virtue and if there is anything praiseworthy-meditate on these things.

    Jesus Christ is the truth! All He ever spoke was truth. His word is truth. We should all be meditating on His Word! When you meditate on His word, your mind takes on new thoughts, new behaviors, and new attitudes. You start thinking on things that are pure, lovely, holy, just, things of good nature. You forget about the negatives of life. It's time to think on Godly - things! If you find yourself thinking on other things, ask the Lord to change your thought life.

    People can clearly know what it means to think about pure and positive things. When I think of lovely and pure, I think of a beautiful woman, a bride and virgin. I think of my beautiful wife because she is lovely! I also think of people that can move other people. They usually are of good report, which means they are likable and are in good standing with people. There is nothing but good things to say about these people.

Are you likable? Experience the impact of Godly thinking. Godly thinking does not get off course. Godly thinking stays focused. Thoughts of love enter your mind and you make right decisions

Having a good report is powerful because it affects others. You always want to have good relationships with others.

There is a God of peace that leads us. He has a way of working those peaceful thoughts in our behaviors throughout the day.

CHAPTER 6
A TRANSFORMED MAN

ROMANS 12:1-2: I beseech you therefore, brethren, by the mercies of God, that ye present your bodies a living sacrifice, holy, acceptable unto God, which is your reasonable service. And be not conformed to this world: but be ye transformed by the renewing of your mind, that ye may prove what is that good, and acceptable, and perfect, will of God.

A man transformed by God is no longer of this world. He is in the world, but not of it. He is now a sanctified, Holy Ghost filled man! He is a Kingdom man because God called him and made him over!

I always hated when Dracula movies came on for many reasons. First of all, it was so dark and evil. Secondly, Dracula would seduce women of his liking so he could bite her and transform her into his Dracula Bride. In other words, he wanted to bring her on the dark side for evil. And He wanted to make her like him, a vampire. He wanted her almost as a sacrifice.

The devil is similar to the Dracula character, but worse. He seduces people to make them sacrifices in his kingdom. People give s themselves over to his seductive spirit. Most people do not recognize the tricks of the evil one. We need Jesus in order to resist being drawn any deeper into Satan's kingdom. May you be rescued right now from the grips of the devil and his demons. Repeat this right now! "Lord Jesus, I surrender to you at this very moment. I repent to you and ask that you come into my heart at this moment. I believe you died for my sin and rose on the third day by the power of God. I accept you as Lord in my heart. Thank you. In Jesus's name. Amen. "

Men must be transformed by the renewing of their minds to get through all attacks. They need to walk in the spirit of Jesus Christ. Be anointed from head to feet! Every man needs a prayer life. It is his duty to protect his wife and children from the enemy. He must be transformed and use the word of God daily for strength, power and his weapon of authority!

Man must present himself to God as a living sacrifice. God does not need a dead sacrifice from you. Jesus paid the price. He was the sacrifice for all mankind. God wants you to live in the spirit and be witnesses on the earth.

You will have the authority to pray and break curses and seductive spirits when you see them approaching your wife. Yes, you guessed it. Men have seductive spirits, as well.

CHAPTER 7
GOD'S GIFTS TO MAN

1 CORINTHIANS 12:4-11: There are different kinds of gifts, but the same Spirit. There are different kinds of service, but the same Lord. There are different kinds of working, but the same God works all of them in all men. Now to each one the manifestation of the Spirit is given for the common good. To one there is given through the Spirit the message of wisdom, to another the message of knowledge by means of the same Spirit, to another faith by the same Spirit, to another gifts of healing by that one Spirit, to another miraculous powers, to another prophecy, to another distinguishing between spirits, to another speaking in different kinds of tongues, and to still another the interpretation of tongues. All these are the work of one and the same Spirit, and he gives them to each one, just as he determines. The body is a unit, though it is made up of many parts; and though all its parts are many, they form one body. So it is with Christ. For we were all baptized by one Spirit into one body whether Jews or Greeks, slave or free and we were all given the one Spirit to drink.

Football season and the holiday seasons are times that get more people stirred up, perhaps than any other. It is fun to watch people with explosive talents. There are also other times of the year such as spring break and Mardi Gras that attract college students and much of the general population. These two events spark rampant sin. It's seen as party time, which results in devastating outcomes for many. There is still hope that the Lord will change hearts and transform people to serve Him.   NFL players dig deep with all their might to show their gift of running, catching, passing, blocking and even tackling another player of the opposite team. There is nothing wrong with that kind of raw talent. Some are the best of the best running backs in College and NFL football. If there is anyone who enjoys watching a winning football team that would be me. The point is that talents and gifts are to be used and expressed to their fullest potential.

    The Apostle Paul teaches us in Corinthians 12. There are nine spiritual gifts in this passage that God has made available to every Christian If fact, God wants every man to be aware and receive the gift that He has for him. The points of these gifts remind us that we are empowered by God to make a difference. The Apostle Paul did not delay in using the gifts that God gave him. He was filled with the Holy Spirit and on fire to use his gifts after being converted.

It is evident that one of his gifts was the message of wisdom and another gift was the message of knowledge. His preaching was superior and bold with fire (Holy Spirit) behind it. The evidence is the Gospel. We know this to be true because the Apostle Paul wrote two-thirds of the gospel which is knowledge and wisdom from above.

The Apostle explains that God simply gives these gifts as He determines. Then He makes them available for those who will choose to serve Him. If you are not ready and mature enough, He may withhold it until you are ready to be a true servant. The Christian does not decide which gift they want. God decides on your gift. We may desire and ask, but ultimately, it is up to Him. You just receive the gift. Make no mistake there are more gifts in the Bible besides these. Please see 1 Corinthians chapters 12-14; Romans 12; Ephesians 4 and 1 Peter 4. You are under God's craftsmanship and authority to use these gifts. Search God for more in your life. Search for God to get the maximum use of your gifts Keep in mind that God wants us to always know that Jesus is our gift first and foremost in this life and everlasting life (1 Corinthians 12:1-11).

CHAPTER 8
OVERCOME YOUR IDENTITY CRISIS

MATTHEW 16

Michelle C. McGregor admired her father because he always picked her up when she fell and always helped her to focus on who she really is as a person. This is just what a father does when it comes to sons and daughters. He picks them up!

In college, Michelle was not content just taking classes. She wanted more in life. She wanted to have fun and take on a new identity. She wanted to be a part of the crowd and join the other girls in groups on campus. She pledged into a sorority. But she experienced an emotional problem because her so called sorority sisters made her do the unthinkable. She had to go room to room visiting guys to get points and make it through the pledge giving sexual favors to each guy. She was forced to have sex and it changed her life. She was rushed to the hospital and then came back home when her father was faced with her emotional and physical crisis. It was his love that brought her back in touch to reality and the love of Jesus Christ. She remembered how her dad would always remind her that her identity signified strength to overcome anything. It was a good thing she was a Christian and her father was there for her! Are you there for your children and family? The horror in Michelle's life was just the beginning. She contracted a sexual disease from one or more of those partners during that pledge. Her biggest challenge was the reality of contracting HIV, and then full blown aids. You guessed it right! Things got worse. There was so much pain in her life.

Jesus is the only answer for everything we will encounter. Stick with Him no matter where you go in life! You need Jesus always; in the worst of times and the best of times.

Jesus asks many questions in Matthew 16:13."Whom do men say that I the Son of man am?" The response is located in Matthew 16:14 which says, " And they said, Some say that thou art the John the Baptist: some, Elias; and others Jeremias, or one of the prophets" Jesus asks another question, Matthew 16:15 "He saith unto them, But whom say ye that I am?" In Matthew 16:16, it says, "And Simon Peter answered and said, thou art the Christ, the Son of the living God." In Matthew 16:17 scripture says, And Jesus answered and said unto him. Blessed art thou, Simon Barjona: for flesh and blood had not revealed this unto you, but my Father which is in heaven (Matthew 16:13-17)." Jesus said in Matthew 16:18 And I say unto thee, That thou art Peter, and upon this rock I will build my church; and the gates of hell shall not prevail against it (Matthew 16:13-18)."

Jesus reminds us that He is responsible for building the church. In the passage above, Jesus points out that just as Peter proclaimed Jesus's identity, Jesus comes right back and reveals Peter's identity. In verse 18, Jesus said, and I say also unto thee, thou are Peter and upon this rock, I will build my church, and the gates of hell shall not prevail against it. Jesus is the head of the church. He selects men to lead God's ministries.

In Matthew Chapter 4, Jesus was in the wilderness and the devil tried to tempt Him by saying if you are the Son of God turn these stone into bread. In verse 4 the response to the devil was "But he answered and said, It is written, Man shall not live by bread alone, but by every word that proceedeth out of the mouth of God Matthew 4:4. The enemy's goal was to make Jesus sin and lose his identity. He wanted Jesus to bow down to Him by offering Jesus things in the following verses Matthew 4:1-11.

    Jesus has a specific destiny for your life. He wants you to start walking in that direction, today. You must know your identity in Jesus Christ. Do not allow the enemy to trick you and steal your identity and God's plan for your life. The devil will play with your mind in an effort to pull you from Jesus's Kingdom to his kingdom of darkness. God's plan is to bless you and prosper you in Jesus Christ. He wants you to help people find their true identities. The Lord has already set it up for you. All you need to do at this point is to start moving in His direction and believe God for the outcome. The timing has been established along with the purpose. Because Peter identified with Jesus, the Lord made him leader over the church. Can you imagine the powerful preaching that went forth out of Peter because he knew who the Lord was and who he was? It was powerful enough to change lives throughout the world.

CHAPTER 9
PRAYER BREAKS PRISON FOUNDATIONS!

ACTS 16:25-26: But at midnight Paul and Silas were praying and singing hymns to God, and the prisoners were listening to them. Suddenly there was a great earthquake, so that the foundations of the prison were shaken, and immediately all the doors were opened and everyone's chains were loosed.

God never intended for men to be behind prison bars (locked up) permanently! We were made to live in a paradise until sin came on the scene.

Paul and Silas were persecuted because they were men of God. This was a witness strategy! God wants men to break every bar and stronghold in whatever mindset and prison you are experiencing in life. Whatever has you on lock down, break it! Break the old things from your past that surfaces to make you feel unworthy! Break the old rules that keep you tied down! Break the traditional man-made rules! Break that Pharisaical mentality! They did not want to follow Jesus. They were high-minded, prideful and jealous-spirited people. Rebuke it in the name of Jesus! Men, God want you to be strengthened in His might! Prayer and praise breaks all prisons, bondages, and barriers! Men that praise God can really make a difference in breaking prison bars. Don't remain locked in prison in your own mind. Don't allow drugs, gang violence and other temptations get a hold on you and damage you any further. Don't allow anything to put you in a prison! You can recover from any bad experience with God on your side.

Two men were in prison (locked up) together. They praised God and caused the power of God to take action. Praise not only freed these men. Praise shook the concrete slab, the bars, the shackles, the chains, and the other prisoners, even the guard. This means that praise can affect the very foundation of a man's life. Whatever sin holds you hostage, the God of the Universe who hears your praise, can set you free. Just take a look at Paul and Silas and their actions at midnight. You might feel like bad addictions, wrong people or wrong behavior took you from God. But it's not too late. Today, stand up as a man and get God in your heart, spirit and soul. Ask God to take away all those things that imprisoned your mind. You need to become a man after God's own heart even like king David. Take on the attitude of Paul and Silas. They made their minds up that no evil would prevail over their lives. Praise God and ask Him to break every chain off of you. You will never be locked up by the devil again. From now on, be influenced by the Holy Spirit to praise God day and night. Be influenced by God to bless your family. Release every sin in the name of Jesus: drug use, pornography, adultery, witchcraft, Ouija boards, and psychic readings. Pray right now and praise Him.

CHAPTER 10
DELIVERANCE OUT OF BONDAGE!

EXODUS 5:1-5: Afterward Moses and Aaron went in and told Pharaoh, "Thus says the LORD God of Israel: 'Let My people go, that they may hold a feast to me in the wilderness.' And Pharaoh said, "Who is the LORD, that I should obey His voice to let Israel go? I do not know the LORD, nor will I let Israel go." So they said, "The God of the Hebrews has met with us. Please, let us go three days' journey into the desert and sacrifice to the LORD our God, lest He fall upon us with pestilence or with the sword." Then the king of Egypt said to them, "Moses and Aaron, why do you take the people from their work? Get back to your labor.

Thousands like Anna Richards welcome witchcraft and demons, into their homes to exercise their evil gifts. It happens so subtly that without a discerning spirit, you can miss it. One day the spirit got on Anna and made her strip her clothes off. After running into the street naked and being subdued by the police, she woke up in an institution. She never realized how she got there, until a year later. Her parents convinced her of what had happened to her. Jesus came into her life and she stopped entertaining the devil through people performing witchcraft in her house. When saw the video of her behavior, it opened her eyes. Her deliverance came as a result of her opening her heart to Jesus to come in. She stopped allowing controlling spirits to take her mind and life. God does not want anyone holding his people in bondage.

God is the God of deliverance. He opposes a pharaoh type mentality. He doesn't want his people living in an Egypt environment. God never intended and is not responsible for His people living that way. That is exactly why He sent Moses to deliver His people from bondage. God specializes in taking people out of bondage. Once you read the entire account of what happened in Egypt, then you will understand the absolute power and love of God for His people. God does not allow slavery to destroy Christians. In His mysterious and blunt ways, God always gets the attention needed to release His people. He makes a way out of no way. His people walked through the Red Sea. He specializes in turning the impossible into the possible. God delivers whoever calls on the name of Jesus Christ.

CHAPTER 11
JESUS PRAYED FOR HIS MEN!

John 17:6-7 I have manifested your name to the men whom you have given me out of the world. They were yours. You gave them to me, and they have kept your word. Now they have known that all things which you have given me and from you.

Jesus is showing us an example of what we should do for other men. We are to pray for them that the devil does not destroy them because of their blindness. God hears all of Jesus's prayers. We have an advocate for prayer at all times. The Holy Spirit is our helper in so many ways. Nevertheless, in this scripture, Jesus prayed for his disciples. In verse 20, he prayed for all who will believe in Him. He was speaking directly to His Father in Heaven.

Jesus wanted His disciples to be blessed by the Father. He knows all about who we are and our desires. If you are a follower of Christ, you can count on the Holy Spirit's prayers on your behalf. The Lord prays for me and you. He prays for us because He cares. This is a prayer of the High Priest. The Lord prayed for God to keep His disciples strong in difficult times. Since I am under construction, make me a prayer warrior. Take me a man of God under construction and put the anointing of prayer on my lips that I will become an intercessor!

CHAPTER 12
JUSTIFIED BY THE BLOOD

ROMANS 5:8-10: But God demonstrates His own love toward us, in that while we were still sinners, Christ died for us. Much more then, having now been justified by His blood, we shall be saved from wrath through Him. For if when we were enemies we were reconciled to God through the death of His Son much more, having been reconciled we are saved by His life.

Ralph's two best friends became gangsters and begin robbing and getting into confrontations in various cities. When Ralph ran into Steve and Micah in a nearby bank, he did not know his life was about to change. You see, these two had just robbed the bank and Ralph's Father was a security guard inside. The situation heightened when Mr. Davis dashed out the door. They both pulled guns and Mr. Davis had his, but they pointed at Ralph. Ralph's Father quickly jumped in front of him and took seven bullets to the chest, legs and shoulder to save his son's life. This is a demonstration of love. The enemies were later apprehended around the corner.

In the same way, Jesus took our place on the cross by dying for us. We have life today because He laid His down. He saved us by the power of His blood. He loved us then and still does today. We are justified by the blood of the Lamb! Justification means not guilty of any wrong doing in the past or ever. We are no longer guilty of the penalty charged against us. It is like the judge and jury in a courtroom who states your verdict is not guilty! Keep in mind, sin is sin, but grace is grace and we abound in His grace. Nothing is stronger than His blood, love, grace and tender mercies. This is what God offers us every day of our lives. Receive it today, along with all His other blessings.

CHAPTER 13
THE AUTHOR & FINISHER OF MY FAITH

HEBREWS 12:1-2 Therefore we also, since we are surrounded by so great a cloud of witnesses, let us lay aside every weight, and the sin which so easily ensnares us, and let us run with endurance the race that is set before us, looking unto Jesus, the author and finisher of our faith, who for the joy that was set before Him endured the cross, despising the shame, and has sat down at the right hand of the throne of God.

You only have one author and finisher of your faith, Jesus Christ. No other religion controls your faith. Your finished faith is based on the cross. Jesus died once for all of us!

God wants man to persevere in faith and endure trials because the enemy longs to kill, steal, and destroy. The enemy roams around like a roaring lion seeking whom he may devour. But God is on your side! He will close the lions and the demons' mouths.

The Lord our God is always cheering us on; as well as providing strength for life challenges. Man must have God in his life to advance in the Kingdom of God. Every father needs God in order to raise a God-fearing family. This family led by the father in the house will learn to reverence God, no matter what. The hand of God will touch them because the priest in the house has activated his faith. 1 John 4:4 reminds me that "Greater is He who is in me than He who is in the world." We need that attitude of faith. God is constantly building the spirit-filled man and directing his life. God will see this man through his life, as well as his family. We can go the distance faithfully in Jesus Christ. Tell your family and friends that a crown of life awaits them from God. Whatever your circumstance is today, God is watching to see if you will pass the test. He wants to know if you will exercise your faith. We are reminded that man has no authority to stop you from serving God.

Your faith can take you to new levels.

CHAPTER 14
GOD LOOKS AT MAN'S HEART

1 Samuel 16:7-8: But the LORD said to Samuel, "Do not look at his appearance or at his physical stature, because I have refused him. For the LORD does not see as man sees; for man looks at the outward appearance, but the LORD looks at the heart. So Jesse called Abinadab, and made him pass before Samuel. And he said, "Neither has the LORD chosen this one."

Make life count! Make the ministry in you count for something! Jesus is looking at you to see if you will be used by Him. God has already chosen you and you are the right man for the job. The Bible reminds us that God can search us. He already knows us. Remember, God formed us in the womb before the foundations of the world.

God does not look at men the way we look at one another. He sees us with the power of love from His heart. He knows exactly who we are before we even know ourselves. He knows our destiny. He knows exactly who each individual will be in life. When it is all said and done, God knows who will reign in His Kingdom in heaven. When David was being sought after by the Prophet Samuel, God already knew that none of David's brothers would fit the description. Neither of them had the same heart that David had demonstrated before God. God had already chosen David as King and blessed him.

God is looking for you to fill a vital position. God anointed David as King and He was ready to battle any enemy. Allow God to build you up as a man of God after His heart. Just like one does with building blocks, God builds a little at a time. And He is effective. God can build man's heart in the same way. I like to think of it like Iron man. His centerpiece appears to be a constructed component in his chest that functions as the heart of his entire power suit. That particular piece is the key to all of his actions in rescuing and fighting. King David's help was God in his heart! God continues to build man piece by piece: heart, mind, soul, body, spirit, and strength. Let Him reconstruct you as a man after His own heart.

CHAPTER 15
GOD IS LOOKING FOR OBEDIENCE IN MAN!

ROMAN 5:19-21: For as by one man's disobedience many were made sinners, So, also by one man's obedience many will be made righteous. Moreover the law entered that the offense might abound. But where sin abounds, grace abounds much more, so that as sin reigned in death, even so grace might reign through righteousness to eternal life through Jesus Christ our Lord.

God does not want us to get it twisted. He can take a disobedient man, change his heart and make him over. Even though Adam failed God, the Lord still expressed His love in Adam's family and his life. Sin tries to reign in our lives and the only way to defeat its temptation daily is to call on the name of Jesus in prayer. Adam could have prayed to the Father. Adam could have taken his family to a prayer meeting or fasted. Adam had a responsibility to guard his family. Every man has the same responsibility Adam had because of the Lord's order.

In the creation of mankind, God made Adam the strongest of the two vessels. The woman is the weaker vessel according to 1 Peter 3:7. It does not mean she is not strong. It just means that God created man stronger, physically and with authority. It is easier for disobedience to enter man's heart when the vessel is weak and out of alignment with God. We remain in alignment by remaining in Jesus (John 15). Disobedience is the original reason and cause of sin entering the earth, the heart of man and his wife. The first family had stepped off course into disobedience which penalized everyone in creation. Romans 5:14: "Nevertheless death reigned from Adam to Moses, even over those who had not sinned according to the likeness of the transgression of Adam, who is a type of Him who was to come."

Adam was God's first man who was made to walk in obedience but did the opposite. He failed God. Thank God for mercy and the power of forgiveness. God had a plan and it was to send His Son, Jesus who was known as the second Adam. He was obedient to His Father in Heaven. This is also a lesson for all of us. We, too, as God's children must embrace an obedient spirit. Children obey your parents so that your life will be long (Ephesians 6).

CHAPTER 16
GOD CALLED YOU!

HEBREWS 11:8: By Faith Abraham obeyed when he was called to go out to the place in which he would receive as an inheritance. And he went out, not knowing where he was going.

People are called by God. As fast as God calls, some respond to Him and some reject Him. The Apostle was called to go on several missionary journeys and he answered the call. You have to be able to make up your mind as to who you will listen to and follow. The logical and only choice should be God.

Abraham had been with his family for years. When you find yourself staying on the same ground for so many years and no progress has been made, it is time for a change. Sometimes God calls you to help make a change for His purpose. God is looking for a man who has ambition and faith in his heart. Start moving from that place that hinders you, blocks your blessings, purpose, and your gifts. Start looking for that place that God may have spoken of concerning you.

It is time to look over what everybody else said about you and look to the hills from whence cometh your help. Your help comes from the Lord. You might not know exactly where you are going and that is exactly what Abraham experienced when he was called Abram. There were more experiences God had for Abram to encounter. Then God would establish a covenant. Abram answered God and it led to Him being the father of many nations. He became the father of faith! He was a blessed man. When will you obey God? God is calling you to step out. Your wife may have already asked God for forgiveness and surrendered her heart to Him. What about you?

CHAPTER 17
SALVATION IN JESUS CHRIST
SOUL WINNER

ROMANS 10:9-10 that if you confess with your mouth the Lord Jesus and believe in your heart that God has raised Him from the dead, you will be saved. For with the heart one believes unto righteousness, and with the mouth confession is made unto salvation.

Salvation only comes by accepting Jesus into your heart and believing according to Romans 10:9 (above). Jesus is the soul winner and the one who can change your spirit.

A soul winner is someone whose focus is on winning people to Jesus Christ, no matter how the enemy opposes or reject them. A soul winner will still take a stand and preach the word for Jesus.

For example consider this story about Alexus. Her dad had just purchased a car for her. She is happy driving her friends back and forth to school. But one day, Alexus's friend Kim asked her if they could take an alternate route home. Alexus says yes and proceeds with directions from Kim. They get to a red light and Kim's boyfriend comes out of nowhere and stops the car. "Greg, what are you doing?!" Right behind Greg is Russell who has a gun pointed in the back of Greg's head. It quickly changed once Alexus asked him to take the gun off of her little brother. "He is only 16. Put your gun on me if you want to hurt somebody". "Get out of the car, little Ms. Bad stuff." She gets out and Russell says, "Move it that way." He wanted her to go under the bleachers where a room was unlocked and his boys where there. "I will not! You can just shoot me now. I believe in Jesus Christ! What do you believe in?" "Man what's up? You are going to let that little girl tell you what to do"? Alexus said, "You all come out as well; nobody is scared of your behinds. All you can do is shoot people. You and your friends need Jesus in your life. Let me pray for you and your friends! Watch what God does for you!" After Alexus prayed with Kim for Russell to put the gun away, then she and Kim both prayed for Russell and his friends. They all stood at the rear of the car as Alexus prayed. They all accepted Jesus Christ according to Romans 10:9. They became born again and were baptized the following Sunday service. Soul winners make it happen.

CHAPTER 18
A CUP FOR THE WORLD

Luke 22:42 says, "Father, if it is your will, take this cup away from me; nevertheless not my will, but yours, be done." It was God's will that Jesus continue to the mission of salvation. John 1:12-13 states "But as many as received Him, to them He gave the right to become children of God, to those who believe in His name: who were born, not of blood, nor of the will of the flesh, nor of the will of man, but of God.

Jesus paid for our life with His life. We now have access to salvation and the Father through Jesus Christ, even those who once rejected Him.

The love of Jesus Christ makes it possible today for all to come to Him and be saved under the power of His grace and love Ephesians 2:5-8. Allow Jesus Christ to be your safety net for life. No longer do you have to live an insecure and unprotected life.

God wants us to turn our lives over to the Him. He can keep us safe each and every day. Saints, God wants us to be led by His will. Listen to what Jesus said in His darkest hour in preparation for the cross. He asked the Father if there is another way, take this cup only if it be your will. This cup is a crucified death. This would be the only way to salvation. Jesus reminds us of the power that comes from God's will! We must be men of God who allow God's will to lead us on the right path. It requires that we have a surrendered spirit like Jesus displayed to His Father. His sacrifice of physical death was necessary to save God's people. Jesus took on the wrath of God to save every person in the world. Today, make sure you stop by and worship God every Sunday to glorify Him for defeating the enemy for your sin.

CHAPTER 19
MAN OF GOD, KICK DEMONS OUT!

LUKE 10:18-23: And He said to them, "I saw Satan fall like lightning from heaven. Behold, I give you the authority to trample on serpents and scorpions, and over all the power of the enemy, and nothing shall by any means hurt you. Nevertheless do not rejoice in this, that the spirits are subject to you, but rather rejoice because your names are written in Heaven." In that hour Jesus rejoiced in the Spirit and said, "I thank you, Father, Lord of heaven and earth, that you have hidden these things from the wise and prudent and revealed them to babes.

Mental conditions can affect all people especially soldiers or anyone who experiences something horrific. Demons use mental attacks to destroy people. Get treated by your physician and Father in heaven.

As a man of God you can kick the devil out of your house. Every man belonging to God has the authority to kick demons out of his house! No demon is authorized to lay hands on you, your wife, nor your children. The devil does not have authority.

Luke is talking about demons when he mentions you have authority to trample on serpents and scorpions. They chase and pursue each man to steal his joy and sabotage his life. I like what the singing artists, Mary, Mary put in their song, and they sang it well "It's the God in me!" When they sing that song I am reminded that it's not me that does good. Nevertheless, it's the God whose power moves in me and through me. It is God's power that chase demons off! Jesus loves when you get behind closed doors and fall to your knees and pray because you really go into warfare against principalities. Everybody may not know what you are doing behind closed doors, but God knows. A lot goes on behind closed doors. Speak the word of God "Greater is He in me than he in the world!" You can tell that demon that has been chasing you that the God in you rebukes all manner of evil. In the name of Jesus, go back to the depths of hell. Your company is not allowed. I rejoice because His word has kicked you out of my presence, out of my house, out of my life in the matchless name of Jesus Christ.

Whenever a storm is likely to occur in your community or near your home, your sense of anxiousness may heighten. Lightning may strike and you may hear loud thundering. Lightning can strike some places and leave its marks behind. We usually have vivid memories of those storms that impact our lives. They last for a while and the only way to remove those scars resulting from a storm is through the everlasting power, mercy and grace of our Lord and Redeemer, Jesus Christ. The same God who kicked the devil out of heaven is the same God who can kick the devil out of your home and out of your life. Every time that enemy attempts to return, you need to open your mouth and speak the word of God to rebuke it in Jesus name as well. "Get thee hence Satan in the name of Jesus Christ, I rebuke you. Flee in Jesus name!" Speak with authority!

CHAPTER 20
DON'T LET YOUR FAMILY GO TO HELL!

Luke 16:19-30 "There was a certain rich man who was clothed in purple and fine linen and fared sumptuously every day. But there was a certain beggar named Lazarus, full of sores, who was laid at his gate, desiring to be fed with the crumbs which fell from the rich man's table. Moreover the dogs came and licked his sores. So it was that the beggar died, and was carried by the angels to Abraham's bosom. The rich man also died and was buried. And being in torments in Hades, he lifted up his eyes and saw Abraham afar off, and Lazarus in his bosom. "Then he cried and said, 'Father Abraham, have mercy on me, and send Lazarus that he may dip the tip of his finger in water and cool my tongue; for I am tormented in this flame.

Have you ever seen a house go up in flames? God is showing us that people can also go up in flames! People are self-destructive in so many ways. They allow the enemy to penetrate their minds and hearts. Men, you are to save your family from torment and hell's flames. You have a role to play and a responsibility to help them! Every man should want the best for their families. Do your part as the man and priest of your house. Your goal upfront is to alert your family to receive Jesus as Lord and Savior. Avoid the flames, which are where the torment is taking place.

The word torment means an extreme form of human suffering. However, before the suffering, an opportunity exists to get right with God. Lazarus did not have anything, he was poor and hungry. The rich man was supposed to feed him. Brother, the flames were consuming the rich man because of his failure to show compassion. The rich man needed salvation in Jesus Christ. After he denied Lazarus food, God denied him water to cool the flames.

CHAPTER 21
GET READY FOR A PENTECOSTAL MOMENT!

ACTS 2:1-13 When the Day of Pentecost had fully come, they were all with one accord in one place. And suddenly there came a sound from heaven, as of a rushing mighty wind, and it filled the whole house where they were sitting. Then there appeared to them divided tongues, as of fire, and one sat upon each of them. And they were all filled with the Holy Spirit and began to speak with other tongues, as the Spirit gave them utterance. And there were dwelling in Jerusalem Jews, devout men, from every nation under heaven. And when this sound occurred, the multitude came together, and was confused, because everyone heard them speak in his own language. Then they were all amazed and marveled, saying to one another, "Look, are not all these who speak Galileans?

People in Louisiana t rush to Mardi Gras to get what they think is the thrill of a lifetime. I've never been to Mardi Gras. When I was a little boy I heard nothing but horror stories: people stabbing and killing others as they wore masks and costumes as they paraded down the streets of New Orleans.

Be careful about the tricks of the devil to lure you into festivals that seem so innocent. Be careful what you participate in. You do not want future generations to be affected, so pass on the good things to the next and future generations. The stories behind Mardi Gras have some pretty wild claims. Nevertheless, there is no worship of God in any of it. Do not allow the enemy to trick you into worshiping him. He can't wait to destroy your homes, family and the city with great devastation. God delights in blessing His people. So don't turn your back on Him.

God does the opposite of the enemy. In the word of God, He gives power and life to those who worship and celebrate Him! The

Greek word for Pentecost is pentekostos which means fifty. This referred to a Jewish Holiday called the Festival of weeks. This comes from Leviticus 23:16 in which the priest is instructed to count seven weeks or fifty days from the end of the Passover to the beginning of the upcoming holiday. The significance of this passage is that the tongues of fire rested on each person who was directed by Jesus to go there and wait. These followers of Jesus Christ were filled with the spirit and empowered to work the ministry under the authority of Jesus Christ. The Holy Spirit rested on each person God wants us to read Acts 2:1-2 to be aware of what He has available for His people.

You will not be empowered by the Holy Spirit at a Mardi Gras. You will find people that call up demon spirits over you and your children. My question to you is will you choose to worship Jesus Christ or demon spirits at home and in Mardi Gras. Avoid trying to impress people! Don't worry about trying to have a good time at demonic events. Start serving and worship God. Start seeking a Pentecostal moment to receive the infilling of the Holy Spirit.

CHAPTER 22
UNDER GOD'S AUTHORITY

JOHN 16:5-15: "But now I go away to Him who sent me, and none of you asks me, 'Where are you going?' But because I have said these things to you, sorrow has filled your heart. Nevertheless I tell you the truth. It is to your advantage that I go away; for if I do not go away, the Helper will not come to you; but if I depart, I will send Him to you. And when He has come, He will convict the world of sin, and of righteousness, and of judgment: of sin, because they do not believe in me; of righteousness, because I go to my Father and you see me no more; of judgment, because the ruler of this world is judged. "I still have many things to say to you, but you cannot bear them now. However, when He, the Spirit of truth, has come, He will guide you into all truth; for He will not speak on His own authority, but whatever He hears He will speak; and He will tell you things to come. He will glorify me, for He will take of what is mine and declare it to you. All things that the Father has are mine. Therefore I said that He would take of mine and declare it to you.

Learning to live under the authority of God is easier than you think. You live under God's authority when you obey Him and demonstrate your love toward Him by helping other people. You can live even better under God's authority by having a humble spirit.

The Holy Spirit comes to help you live under God's authority. He helps you to separate the good from the bad. The Centurion soldier understood authority because he had men under his authority. Yet this leader of soldiers understood that Jesus was far greater than anyone else. He asked Jesus to just speak the word that his servant would be healed.

In authority, there must be times to convict the world of sin, righteousness and judgment.

CHAPTER 23
A SET MIND

1 Corinthians 2:16 for who hath known the mind of the Lord, that he may instruct him? but we have the mind of Christ.
Phil 2:5 Let this mind be in you, which was also in Christ Jesus.

Humility is the attribute we see in Jesus (Philippians 2). This is the attitude that God loves to see in His spirit-filled men. He expects it because He displayed it in every aspect of His life on earth. A set mind reveals the character of Jesus. When you allow your mind to be set by the Holy Spirit, changes and blessings occur. Then you can be led and expect to be on the receiving end of those blessings. In verses 8-10, Jesus humbled himself to the death of the cross. He did it out of His Love for the Father.

Set your mind on a mission that will count in changing someone else's life. When I first started in the ministry, I set my mind on Jesus first. I also wanted to impress my wife and children by serving God every week in church. I wanted them to see that God had changed me for real! I preached the gospel to impress the Lord, Jesus Christ. I just wanted to be pleasing in His sight. God is too good not to impress. I also wanted my father and my mother to know that the Holy Spirit was working in me to preach to give God the glory as a witness. I was setting my mind on Him.

We need to always allow God to make our minds like His. We should request Him to refresh our minds when we get off course or need a helping hand. If we have to have a total makeover, so be it. You should desire the mind of Christ if you desire to operate in His kingdom. It is important to understand that thought patterns can block blessings in your life. Nothing can stop the move of God in your life. However, your mind needs to be open to Him always. He will reflect Himself through you to others. He will reveal things to you in order to bless you. Set your heart and mind on God. We can have the mind of Christ. Never let any demon or person tell you otherwise. Praise and Glorify His name (1 Corinthians 2:1-16).

CHAPTER 24
MAN FINDING PEACE IN GOD

PHIL 4:7: and the peace of God, which surpasses all understanding, will guard your hearts and minds through Christ Jesus.

A man needs peace in God. Otherwise, he will stay confused, lost, violent and a person who will commit pure acts of evil. However, when a man gets peace, his life is settled and blessed like no other. Every man should strive to be a peace maker as in Matthew 5. Peace makes the Father in the house relax. He sets the entire tone in the house. The wife is joyful. Sons and daughters are happy. Life is good!

Man was created to walk in peace. Many men are searching for peace today because it was lost in the Garden of Eden when sin entered the world. Today, if your life is in an uproar, you can easily calm it down with Jesus in your life.

Jesus calmed the raging sea with his disciples on the boat (Mark 4:35-40). He spoke it and peace was in the atmosphere and the sea. Jesus has all power in His hand. Men were created to walk in peace.

If you are dealing with a son who is running with gangs and smoking drugs, robbing people, breaking and entering and living on the edge, you need to settle down and get the peace of God in your life. Jesus wants us to know His peace. With it, our lives, families, churches, and nations can be transformed and revitalized.

With a peaceful heart, you can lower your defenses enough to let some beautiful woman and a friend inside. You don't always have to be on the defense. The peace of God guards your heart. The purpose is to reveal God's love toward us so that we can release love to others. When we have that kind of love usually it signifies that we have absolute peace that comes from God.

CHAPTER 25
MAN FINDING GRACE IN GOD'S EYES

GENESIS 6:5-8: Then the LORD saw that the wickedness of man was great in the earth, and that every intent of the thoughts of his heart was only evil continually. And the LORD was sorry that He had made man on the earth, and He was grieved in His heart. So the LORD said, "I will destroy man whom I have created from the face of the earth, man and beast, creeping thing and birds of the air, for I am sorry that I have made them." But Noah found grace in the eyes of the LORD.

Athletes work to express the best of their talent and ability to catch the coach and/or scout's eyes. We always compared our letters from colleges. It built us up at times.

A football player has his eyes on the Heisman trophy and later he awaits the call to find out which NFL team will recruit him. You see each player knew that someone (a scout) had been watching and observing his skills and moves on the field every week. He was observed to see if he could follow a coach and make his performance shine in the eyes of everyone in the stadium. If he could, it would be payoff time.

God has his eyes on you! He is looking for something unique in every man that represents His glory. Can you imagine how Noah must have felt when God recognized him as a man of grace in his eyes? Noah's story tells us that God was not pleased with people on this earth because sin had become rampant in the heart of man. They had allowed sin to penetrate their hearts in every imaginable way. Their minds and hearts were totally evil in God's sight. They had the worst imaginations and their minds were constantly thinking evil. Through all of that, God still found a man that He could trust. God found a man called Noah. Noah found grace in the eyes of the Lord. God found grace in one man because of his obedience and willingness to listen to the voice of God. That is exactly what believers in the world today should desire. We want to find grace in the eyes of the Lord. Thank God that He has sent Jesus to redeem us. It was Jesus who saw something in us through His Father's eyes.

CHAPTER 26
THE POWER OF HIS WORD

HEBREWS 4:12: The word of God is living and powerful, and sharper than any two-edged sword, piercing even to the division of soul and spirit, and of joints and marrow, and is a discerner of the thoughts and intents of the heart.

Even today in the Armed Forces swords have specific meanings. When you think of the term, you think about fighting. God's word is more powerful than all the swords combined. It has power beyond our imagination. God's word has revelation and power. It cannot fail.

The word of God is living and more powerful than anything you can imagine in existence. Fortunately for us, the Word, Jesus, is living in us. It is the word that examines us and encourages us to see who we really are. It is the word that penetrates our lives. He reveals to us who we are, what we need to do to make a change in our lives. Some people have conditions that they are not even aware of until they visit a hospital.

If you want to become better through the power of healing, you need faith and the word of God. If you want to communicate better, you need the word to go out and not return void. The word can straighten you out and every crooked place. The word will make enemies your foot stool. If you want to become a priestly man, the answer is in the word. The word will work out things in your life that you could have never imagined. Ask God to do surgery on you. He is able to change your identity with His word. He can do anything but fail. He is all-powerful.

It was the Word in Genesis, the beginning that created the world. When God spoke it was power to create life. The universe came into existence. All power is in the word of God. In John 1, the Bible describes Jesus as the word. The scripture reads in John 1:1-2 IN the beginning was the Word and the Word was with God, and the Word was God. The same was in the beginning with God. John tells us who is the word, where did the word come from, and who the word is. There is much impact in the life of the believer when He or she reads about the word of God.

CHAPTER 27
A HOLY SPIRIT FILLED MAN

Acts 2:4: And they were all filled with the Holy Spirit and began to speak with other tongues, as the Spirit gave them utterance.

God enables us to speak with authority because He fills us with his Holy Spirit. Speaking in tongues is evidence that a person is filled and influenced by the Holy Ghost. It is important to accept Jesus Christ in your heart according to Romans 10:9-10 to receive salvation. You also receive the Holy Spirit at the time you receive Jesus Christ even if you did not speak tongues at that moment. Jesus, His Father and the Holy Spirit are one. When we are filled with the Holy Spirit, we speak God's word with authority and power. Jesus speaks to the storm and tells it, "Peace be still." He does it because He is filled in the Spirit to say the least; He is the Son of God. Joshua told the people to go around the Walls of Jericho seven times and shout. Then the walls came down.

The power of life and death is in the tongue. This is to inspire someone who may have a calling to serve God. "Lord, thank you for filling me with the Holy Spirit. My life has not been the same since you saved me and filled me. I pray that the power of your word is manifested throughout the earth for your purpose".

CHAPTER 28
A MAN OF FAITH

HEBREWS 11:1-3 Now faith is the substance of things hoped for, the evidence of things not seen. For by it the elders obtained a good testimony. By faith we understand that the worlds were framed by the word of God, so that the things, which are seen, were not made of things that are visible.

Every year a film producer produces a new Avengers, Batman, Super Man or Captain American movie to show our society the power of superheroes. As old as I am, I still get those wonderful feelings of excitement from the heroic acts in those movies. One week, I imagine I am the man of steel. The next week I am Iron Man. I just can't make up my mind which one I want to be for sure, maybe all of them. They are fun to watch because of two primary reasons. Primarily, they demonstrate ultimate confidence and faith. Secondly, they always get the victory by saving lives and defeating the enemy!

I remember seeing Superman stop the fastest locomotive by flying to the front and pushing it in the opposite direction or just lifting it with shear strength. I have had some of the wildest thoughts about super heroes. What if they all got together, the Dark Knight, Superman, Super Friends, Spider-Man, the Incredible Hulk, Flash, Green Hornet, Hercules, the Transformers, the men of 300, an Olympic Gold Medalist and a new character that I invented, The Transformation Man in a big box office production to save the world. I hope someday these movies project superheroes bringing people to salvation. This is the job of the Transformation Man. The Transformation Man is part preacher and part superhero. The actions of the superheroes can have a positive impact on the Christian world as well as secular groups.

Faith gets God's attention because it demonstrates our dependence on Him. The worlds were formed by faith. A man with faith steps into the supernatural and walks under the Holy Ghost's influence. Use your faith now! God can do all of what every superhero can do and more. Jesus has defeated that old enemy! Every Christian is supposed to walk stronger each day like a superhero. Take back your house, your heart, your dignity and your mind! Take back whatever the enemy has stolen from you. Take everything back because you belong to God. Step into your destiny which includes victory with God. You are a faith fighter and a Man of God.

When the saints come together, we can take back the city. Imagine the power of God placed in you! Today, you can tell all of your friends, relatives and your wife that you are a Man of Faith. You can step out on faith when God calls you, like Abraham did. Faith is a weapon itself. Not only do you have faith, Jesus has faith and is at the right hand of the Father in heaven. When the Holy Spirit goes to the Father on our behalf, His faith is unleashed and God blesses us. Keep activating your faith within! Turn the faith up every day to get a new victory. In Jesus name, Amen!

CHAPTER 29
I WILL TRUST GOD

JOB 13:13-15: Why do I take my flesh in my teeth, and put my life in my hands? Though He slay me, yet will I trust Him. Even so, I will defend my own ways before Him. He also shall be my salvation, for a hypocrite could not come before Him.

No matter what happens, trust God! The things that come at you might get scary! Trust God regardless! Job expresses the need to continue with God on his side. No matter how bad things get, you will still need Jesus to comfort you and restore your life. It starts with trusting God and believing in Him. Trust is essential in every relationship. Believing is a must! In each marriage, the wife and husband trust each other. God wants us to trust Him. Tell the Lord that you will trust Him in all things.

The enemy specializes in trying to rob God's people of joy, faith and peace. It looked like Job had every reason to turn his back on God. The enemy was trying to make him stop trusting God. His wife even told him to curse God and die. That was an awful thing to tell your husband.

Don't allow fear and a hard blow run you away from God. Life deals us blows. It can seem impossible to handle a heavy load. But God is there in the midst of your confusion, lack of trust and doubt. God is there to help reinstate your faith that you lost because of your crisis. God is there to help hold you up and keep you together. Trust Him.

CHAPTER 30
HE RESTORES LIFE

EZEKIEL 37:4 Again He said to me, Prophesy to these bones, say to them, O dry bones, hear the word of the Lord!

What would you do if God placed you in a valley with the anointing all over you? Would you help to restore a person, a family member, a friend when God instructs you to do so? You can take the initiative to do it! In this case, the Lord specifically told Ezekiel to prophesy over dead bones. God put His anointing on Ezekiel to speak life to dead bones. He gave Ezekiel the gift to prophesy! Let us take a look at the power of God through Ezekiel's mission.

The Lord told Ezekiel to speak over an army of dead bones to raise them up. This is super faith and an anointing of God. Can you see the picture? Here lies an entire nation of dead bones. God's power is flowing through your words to speak and the bones return to life. God wants men to be restored back to life and back to Him! God will bring whatever He wants back to life. If it is dead, God is able to restore.

Lazarus was dead and Jesus called him back to life. A little girl was dead and Jesus brought her back to life. Elijah used his anointing to bring a little boy back to life. God has the power to bring people back to life. We, as Christians, believe in the resurrection of Jesus from the dead. God raised Him up and defeated death! God is showing us what He can do with anyone who needs to be restored back to life.

A woman was accused of making false financial reports at work. Her boss clamped down on her. She denied responsibility but he did not believe her because the evidence pointed in her direction.

She had to go to court and it appeared that the judge did not believe her, either. She went to another panel for finance review and it was hard. Three days later, her son was in a car accident and on life support. Five months earlier, her husband had left her for another woman. Now her job was on the line. What must she do? Prayer is always the answer. When we go through the valley, we need to realize that God knows everything about us even when we want to lie down and die. God may have sent you to church so that the pastor can prophesy over your life. He can preach restoration and your life be restored. You will know it because God will give you twice as much as what you lost!

CHAPTER 31
JESUS IS THE WORD

JOHN 1:1-12: In the beginning was the Word, and the Word was with God, and the Word was God. He was in the beginning with God. All things were made through Him, and without Him nothing was made that was made. In Him was life, and the life was the light of men. And the light shines in the darkness, and the darkness did not comprehend it. There was a man sent from God, whose name was John. This man came for a witness, to bear witness of the Light, that all through him might believe. He was not that Light, but was sent to bear witness of that Light. That was the true Light, which gives light to every man coming into the world. He was in the world, and the world was made through Him, and the world did not know Him. He came to His own, and His own did not receive Him. But as many as received Him, to them He gave the right to become children of God, to those who believe in His name:

On that one evening, it all came to light. I took Lamar to his baptism class around 1994 while living in Massachusetts. He needed the class before Pastor Palmer would baptize him. I had just found my way back to Jesus Christ and I was on fire. Nevertheless, I still had more to be revealed to me at my young stage in the ministry. Well God made this very scripture illuminate that night as the Pastor was teaching it. I had never experienced scripture illuminating before. I was not about to tell anyone just yet. They probably would have thought I was crazy.

Later I would tell some people as a witness to His marvelous power and blessing in my life. The Pastor simply explained how Jesus bridged the gap! Jesus placed a bridge between His people and God. Because He had redeemed us in the blood, we could approach God now in Jesus. John makes it perfectly clear that Jesus is the Word. Not only is He the Word, everything was made by the Word of God. It made sense to me because Jesus is the light. When he reveals Himself, he uses His light. He is the light of the world so that people can see Him in His word and a manifestation of His power. People can see Jesus in His saints. Amen. I received Jesus and begin to preach the gospel. I was telling everyone about Jesus.

CHAPTER 32
A NEW MAN RAISED UP IN CHRIST!

ROMANS 6:1-8: What shall we say, then? Shall we go on sinning so that grace may increase? By no means! We died to sin; how can we live in it any longer? Or don't you know that all of us who were baptized into Christ Jesus were baptized into his death? We were therefore buried with him through baptism into death in order that, just as Christ was raised from the dead through the glory of the Father, we too may live a new life. If we have been united with him like this in his death, we will certainly also be united with him in his resurrection. For we know that our old self was crucified with him so that the body of sin might be done away with, that we should no longer be slaves to sin because anyone who has died has been freed from sin. Now if we died with Christ, we believe that we will also live with him.

When I was given the assignment to draw a set of blueprints in college, I was shocked at the level of obedience and discipline required to complete such an assignment. There were some things that I was unfamiliar with that were extremely necessary to accomplish each blueprint project. I was not experienced by any means. My skills were undeveloped. So I had to learn quickly if I wanted to survive in that particular course. For most assignments, you needed to take it home to complete it with a fast turn - around.

I did not understand the power of design. But, God has so much amazing power in every imaginable way. Truly His design of life is in us, as His creation. God, our Father, has the blueprint of creation in His hand. The scripture above reminds us that we are partakers of the resurrection because we believe that He died and rose from the grave. The believer shows the world their faith in the resurrection by receiving baptism because it symbolizes the death, burial and resurrection. Each candidate for baptism steps into the water and then is immersed into the water and raised up. This new convert or believer rise to a new life. The Pastor explains what baptism means every time someone turns their life over to Jesus and makes a commitment. God is looking for a new man in every household. When you become a new man in Jesus Christ, demons may chase you, but shackles from bondage are broken, life is filled with blessings. Marriages are stronger, life feels real. The spirit of obedience is present. God makes you a witness to plant seed and gather the harvest. When you become a new man, you can't help but to worship God and give Him your time because you are united with Him and identify the resurrection of Jesus in your heart. You become a sanctified priest of the most High God.

CHAPTER 33
THE RESURRECTION

MATTHEW 28: 1-8 Now after the Sabbath, as the first day of the week began to dawn, Mary Magdalene and the other Mary came to see the tomb. And behold, there was a great earthquake, for an angel of the Lord descended from heaven, and came and rolled back the stone from the door, and sat on it. His countenance was like lightning, and his clothing as white as snow. And the guards shook for fear of him, and became like dead men. But the angel answered and said to the women, "Do not be afraid, for I know that you seek Jesus who was crucified. He is not here; for He is risen, as He said. Come, see the place where the Lord lay. And go quickly and tell His disciples that He is risen from the dead, and indeed He is going before you into Galilee; there you will see Him. Behold, I have told you." So they went out quickly from the tomb with fear and great joy, and ran to bring His disciples word.

Jesus is raised from the dead and proof is in the word and the shroud of Turin. You can ask the entire scientific team that studied the shroud. I want to tell you today that only God could have rolled the stone away and raised Jesus up. Imagine stepping inside the tomb and witnessing God raising Jesus up from the dead. Keep that thought! That thought alone will transform you and make you a believer in Jesus Christ. You have stones in your life that need to be moved by the power of Jesus. He already removed the sin that was entangling all of us. But we still need to have Jesus in our lives to remove stones that keep rolling back in place. We need Jesus to remove the stones of hatred, jealousy, disobedience, pride, and lack of love. We need to have a free spirit to worship Him in the beauty of His Holiness. Jesus desires that we be set free. There is nothing too hard for God to roll back from your life. He rolled back death and rose from the dead. He lives in heaven with his eyes on everyone full of love, joy and power.

CHAPTER 34
GOD SET YOU FREE FROM EGYPT!

EXODUS 12:12-16 "For I will pass through the land of Egypt on that night, and will strike all the firstborn in the land of Egypt, both man and beast; and against all the gods of Egypt I will execute judgment: I am the LORD. Now the blood shall be a sign for you on the houses where you are. And when I see the blood, I will pass over you; and the plague shall not be on you to destroy you when I strike the land of Egypt. 'So this day shall be to you a memorial; and you shall keep it as a feast to the LORD throughout your generations. You shall keep it as a feast by an everlasting ordinance. Seven days you shall eat unleavened bread. On the first day you shall remove leaven from your houses. For whoever eats leavened bread from the first day until the seventh day, that person shall be cut off from Israel. On the first day there shall be a holy convocation, and on the seventh day there shall be a holy convocation for you. No manner of work shall be done on them; but that which everyone must eat that only may be prepared by you.

The blood would protect all who were covered by it. The lamb's blood had to be on the doorpost of every house so that the destroyer would pass over. When God expressed His judgment, then and only then, would the breaking point be revealed in Pharaoh. God gave Pharaoh one last chance. Pharaoh had such a hardened heart, so hard that even after God took his first-born, he still didn't want to be in the will of God. You would think that life was precious to Pharaoh since he was a ruler. But evidently, he did not care and relied on his evil spirit. Pharaoh sent his army to chase God's people in the desert. God revealed two more miracles to Pharaoh. He made a whirlwind of fire to block the army from God's people and the red sea. Moses held the rod up and the sea opened and the people walked through to the other side. Pharaoh's army went into the red sea and God closed the sea on his army. It was finally then when Pharaoh was convinced that God is God. Moses' God is God and there is no other like Him.

CHAPTER 35
A MAN WITH A DREAM

GEN 45:3- 13: Then Joseph said to his brothers, "I am Joseph; does my father still live?" But his brothers could not answer him, for they were dismayed in his presence. And Joseph said to his brothers, "Please come near to me." So they came near. Then he said: "I am Joseph your brother, whom you sold into Egypt. But now, do not therefore be grieved or angry with yourselves because you sold me here; for God sent me before you to preserve life. For these two years the famine has been in the land, and there are still five years in which there will be neither plowing nor harvesting. And God sent me before you to preserve posterity for you in the earth, and to save your lives by a great deliverance. So now it was not you who sent me here, but God; and He has made me a father to Pharaoh, and lord of all his house, and a ruler throughout all the land of Egypt. "Hurry and go up to my father, and say to him, 'thus says your son Joseph: "God has made me lord of all Egypt; come down to me, do not tarry.

    A vision is a picture in the mind of men. A vision allows you to see future success down the road. God reveals visions and dreams. He reveals a great deal of what He expects and already has purposed for your life. What is your vision? Today is your day to start formulating it. You can do it. Sit down, start writing your dream, mission, desires, goals and/or purpose in life. Ask God what it is that He is revealing to you. Ask Him to help you understand it. God is the answer for you and me to have a successful vision. Is your vision a new ministry? Is it to be a movie star? Is your dream to be an R&B music artist, country artist? Is your desire to be an athlete? You can be a doctor, lawyer, priest, judge, fireman or any specialty you desire to be. Nevertheless, seek God.

It is important that you start seeing yourself in the very moment of that dream. Do you remember Joseph? Joseph was the son of Jacob who had 12 sons. Joseph was betrayed by his brothers, cast into prison, and taunted by Pharaoh's wife to have sexual relationships. Prior to having all the troubles in his life, Joseph had a dream that his brothers and family members would bow before him someday. He had a dream that He would be in a high position of authority granted by God. He became the second highest in command of Egypt. It was a dream and it was the favor of God. Listen, God sent Joseph into Egypt to preserve life. He gave Joseph the wisdom to calculate storing up goods through the famine. Although Joseph had powerful dreams and interpretations of others dreams, he was still a man of action for God. He backed up his words. God is looking for men who are dreamers, yet who can also back up their words through action.

CHAPTER 36
PUT YOUR SOUL IN JESUS'S HANDS!

MATTHEW 16:26: For what profit is it to a man if he gains the whole world, and loses his own soul? Or what will a man give in exchange for his soul?

I am always reminded of Olympians and how they put forth all their energies to win the prize. Their profit is a gold medal, fortune, and fame. They could have been putting their all into the spreading the word of God.

If you are going to be an Olympian, you should put God first. When you win your gold medal, let everyone know that God helped you win your dream of becoming a gold medalist. We should put God in our lives first. Make sure we give God the glory.

You can ask almost anyone to see if they would love being a millionaire or billionaire. The obvious answer is yes! Microsoft and Apple are leading the computer industry in businesses that are valued in the millions and billions. We live in a world where everything revolves around profits and people wanting to get rich quick. You can increase earnings and profits using various strategies. However, do not allow greed to slip in and become the focus in your heart rather than Jesus. Profits can be made in every ministry, business, and in the market place. What makes a man work so hard to get money? It is his desire to get ahead in life and gain recognition beyond his competitors. Don't lose your soul to gain the whole world. Jesus's disciples made a conscience decision that they were going to follow Him (Mark 12). Jesus called them His disciples because they submitted to His authority, teaching and practiced His teachings. Some even wrote the Bible to reflect His words. These men knew what would be their profit. The gain is life in Christ, Jesus. Money does not win souls; Jesus wins souls through His word, Spirit and power. He is the only God and there is not one like Him! Give Him glory! Your life is the best life in Jesus Christ.

CHAPTER 37
WITNESS OF HIS POWER

MATTHEW 17:1-9: Now after six days Jesus took Peter, James, and John his brother, led them up on a high mountain by themselves; and He was transfigured before them. His face shone like the sun, and His clothes became as white as the light. And behold, Moses and Elijah appeared to them, talking with Him. Then Peter answered and said to Jesus, "Lord, it is good for us to be here; if you wish, let us make here three tabernacles: one for you, one for Moses, and one for Elijah." While he was still speaking, behold, a bright cloud overshadowed them; and suddenly a voice came out of the cloud, saying, "This is my beloved Son, in whom I am well pleased. Hear Him!" And when the disciples heard it, they fell on their faces and were greatly afraid. But Jesus came and touched them and said, "Arise, and do not be afraid." When they had lifted up their eyes, they saw no one but Jesus only. Now as they came down from the mountain, Jesus commanded them, saying, "Tell the vision to no one until the Son of Man is risen from the dead."

Jesus allowed Peter, James and John to see Him in the transfiguration. This is powerful because Jesus is establishing and training His disciples. The transfigurations suggest a transformation not only outside but inside as well. First of all, He had to give them something to see in order to witness to the world. Jesus reveals His glory to His disciples in the mountain and at the same time presents two other witnesses of God's divine power, who were prophets from the Old Testament. Moses may have been mentioned because he was caught up to God in His glory. Elijah was one who was caught up to heaven without dying. His picture represents the rapture (1 Thessalonian 4:13-18). It seems that the Lord is expressing that He was pleased with His son, Jesus. Jesus is the fulfillment of the Old Testament, the prophets and the law. He became an obedient witness on earth to people and His Father could bear witness to it. Jesus also proved to show love that is superior to any man on earth. Jesus walked in the glory of His Father on earth and never sinned. He expressed His Fathers will, love and performed miracles by restoring people's lives. Another reason may be that the Lord was expressing the power of witnessing through His chosen prophets of the past, Moses and Elijah. Nevertheless, His emphasis was definitely on the Son of God who did not hesitate to come to earth on a mission (the cross and resurrection) for His Father and become the sacrifice to save the world from God's wrath. God wants His people to know that as they become transformed in their heart, mind, and spirit, they will also be pleasing in God's sight until He returns.

CHAPTER 38
MAN IN WORSHIP TO GOD!

REVELATION 4: 10-12: the twenty-four elders fall down before Him who sits on the throne and worship Him who lives forever and ever, and cast their crowns before the throne, saying: " You are worthy, O Lord, To receive glory and honor and power; For You created all things, And by Your will they exist and were created."

Every man must make it a priority to bow down every day on his knees to the living God. Let Him know that you are serious about your relationship. This picture of the 24 elders giving honor and glory to God in the heavens is impacting. Take a moment and think on this scene.

They understand His majesty and desire to bow down and worship Him. "The twenty four elders fall down before Him. They cast their crowns before the throne, saying you are worthy O' Lord, to receive glory and honor and power." They recognized that he had created all things including that moment of glory. They cast their crowns to show complete submission, worship, reverence and exaltation. God deserves the praise. He holds my soul in His hand. Worship to you O Lord! You are magnified and given all glory forever and ever through eternity. Get ready to worship God when you turn your life over to Jesus. Tell some people you know how He blessed you!

CHAPTER 39
MAN UNDER THE INFLUENCE OF GOD

EPHESIANS 5:17-19: Therefore do not be unwise, but understand what the will of the Lord is. And do not be drunk with wine, in which is dissipation; but be filled with the Spirit, speaking to one another in psalms and hymns and spiritual songs, singing and making melody in your heart to the Lord,

The wine was given as stated in the book of Timothy to help heal stomachaches and other illnesses. Jesus does not want you to get it wrong and think it is okay to drink and get drunk. Drunkenness alters your mental state. You are capable of being completely destructive in your home (as well as on the highway). Alcohol makes you become belligerent and can cause you to become sexually vulnerable to women. Some people will get drunk and never know what dangers they caused themselves and others. Some have gotten drunk and conceived children. It is wrong to become intoxicated. How can you be ready for Jesus if you are drunk? It also causes you to operate under the influence of a substance rather than the influence of the Holy Spirit. If you love God, you will change this habit and behavior. Times have changed and people do not care about you trying to impress them with drinking. Stop telling yourself that you need a drink. Instead tell yourself that you need to be filled with the Spirit and under His anointing. God wants our lives to be influenced by Him and not a substance!

CHAPTER 40
GOD ORDAINED IT!

PSALM 8
O LORD, our Lord,
How excellent is Your name in all the earth,
Who have set Your glory above the heavens!
Out of the mouth of babes and nursing infants
You have ordained strength,
Because of Your enemies,
That You may silence the enemy and the avenger.

When I consider Your heavens, the work of Your fingers,
The moon and the stars, which You have ordained,
What is man that You are mindful of him,
And the son of man that You visit him?
For You have made him a little lower than the angels,
And You have crowned him with glory and honor.

You have made him to have dominion over the works of Your hands; You have put all things under his feet,
All sheep and oxen—
Even the beasts of the field,
The birds of the air,

And the fish of the sea
That pass through the paths of the seas.

O LORD, our Lord,
How excellent is your name in all the earth!

CHAPTER 41
THE CROSS

JOHN 19:31-35: Therefore, because it was the Preparation Day, that the bodies should not remain on the cross on the Sabbath (for that Sabbath was a high day), the Jews asked Pilate that their legs might be broken, and that they might be taken away. Then the soldiers came and broke the legs of the first and of the other who was crucified with Him. But when they came to Jesus and saw that He was already dead, they did not break His legs. But one of the soldiers pierced His side with a spear, and immediately blood and water came out. And he who has seen has testified, and his testimony is true; and he knows that he is telling the truth, so that you may believe

This was the greatest act of love that man has ever known. Jesus's sacrificial act of love on the cross is demonstrative of His extreme selflessness and blessings for mankind. The soldiers pierced His side and blood and water came out. According to most scholars, this represented washing (by the blood) and cleansing power (by the water). This is why my mother cried when all her children were baptized. She was touched by His grace, love and tender mercies. Not only should mothers influence their children, but the man of the house (priest) should make sure his children know the basics of being a Christian. Help them read and learn scriptures such as Mark 1, Luke 1, 2, Romans 10:9-10, John 3:1-10, 1 Corinthians 13, Galatians 5, John 19 and Mark 16. The movie "The Passion of the Christ" was a remarkable depiction of Jesus giving His life for our sin.

I still did not understand it all. Resurrection Day - this was the day that love was demonstrated beyond measure. No other event in history can compare. This is the most critical event that could have ever taken place on earth. This is why every preacher is to preach the cross, grave, and resurrection. The blood of Jesus washed you and me whiter than snow He took our wrath. Read Isaiah Chapters 53:1-7. In verse 7, the word of God says, He was oppressed, and he was afflicted, yet he opened not his mouth: he was brought as a lamb to the slaughter, and as a sheep before her shearers is dumb, so he openeth not his mouth (Isaiah 53:7). We should pick up our cross daily because of our Lord and Savior (Matthew 16:22-25).

Saints if it had not been for the Lord on our side where would we be? We would have had to experience the wrath of God. He died for you and me.

CHAPTER 42
IT IS FINISHED!

JOHN 19:29-30: Now a vessel full of sour wine was sitting there; and they filled a sponge with sour wine, put it on hyssop, and put it to His mouth. So when Jesus had received the sour wine, He said, "It is finished!" And bowing His head, He gave up His spirit.

What is something that you have accomplished to impress the closest people in your life? Was it a college degree? Was it a multi-million dollar business? Was it that you made it to the pros in football, basketball, golf, or the Olympics? Those are superb accomplishments. But nothing compares to Jesus on the cross. His death and resurrection was the most remarkable miracles. Jesus was willing to take on death because of His love for humanity! Jesus spoke saying, "It is finished!" meaning nothing else was required and every human being was purchased. The veil had to split which signified that relationship has been restored to man, so that he might approach God through Jesus.

When we see the cross, we see the most precious commitment to love that has ever existed in time The Lamb was slain for you and me. It is when people truly receive that truth is when change is activated on the inside. When people wear a cross as a symbol, it is a reminder of what Jesus did for a world entrenched in sin. It is a reminder that people have been redeemed. It is evidence that sin was destroyed on the cross by the power of God through His precious Son, Jesus. God destroyed sin in His son's body on the cross. No one or any other sacrifice could take the place of Jesus.

He was and is the only way out of sin. He is the only way to everlasting life. Jesus is the way the truth and the life and He is the only way to the Father.

CHAPTER 43
CURIOUS CREATURES!

ISAIAH 27:1, JOB 41, PSALM 74:14

Some things just blow a person's mind in God's creation. There used to be a debate as to whether dinosaurs were real and were they created by God and so forth. Dinosaur bones were discovered by many scientists in the 1800's. Many scientists have found various bone fragments as evidence of their existence. You can't dispute real life evidence. No one can plant a full replica of a dinosaur deep inside the mountain rock and preserve it for millions of years, except God who is the Creator. The movie Jurassic Park made mega-millions. It is still showing today, all versions are still popular. No wonder God did away with the dinosaurs. Man and dinosaur are not a good mix.

Proof of dinosaurs have been discovered. What sparked this subject was a show called Dinosaur 13 that captured my attention as I was studying another course. The Dinosaur 13 discovery of 1996 fascinated me. A group of researchers from Black Hills Institute just happened to find the dinosaur (T-Rex) at a mountain base. A female accidently found it when she was lost due to heavy fog. She had made two trips around to the same location ending up at the base of that mountain or cliff, so to speak. They called the dinosaur, Sue. That case was a great discovery that lead to court battles and false imprisonment of a good man. Today those dinosaur bones are in a museum.

Whatever God creates, He knows how to handle. When destruction comes your way, God can handle it. The lesson here is that God wants man to be aware of His power to create; and the authority He granted man to have dominion is still available for him today. .

CHAPTER 44
WORSHIP GOD!

REV 7:13: Then one of the elders asked me, these in the white robes who are they, and where did they come? I answered, Sir, you know. And he said, these are they who have come out of the great tribulation; they have washed their robes and made them white in the blood of the Lamb.

John had a vision that allowed him to see in the heavenly realm. God revealed the book of Revelation to him. In fact, he was taken to heaven in the Spirit to see what God wanted to reveal to Him. In that event, John was moved in the spirit, like in a time portal. He was allowed to see chosen people of God dressed in white robes. He was allowed to see the future. Jesus even showed John Himself. He revealed to him, the throne and the fountain that never runs dry. One of the elders in heaven saw John and responded to him. The Elder had identified the thousands and thousands of worshipers as those that came out of the great tribulation. God blessed all of those worshipers and allowed their robes to be washed in the blood of the Lamb.

CHAPTER 45
AUTHORITY TO BIND!

Acts 9:14-18: And here he has authority from the chief priests to bind all who call on your name. But the Lord said to him, "Go, for he is a chosen vessel of mine to bear my name before Gentiles, kings, and the children of Israel. For I will show him how many things he must suffer for my name's sake. And Ananias went his way and entered the house; and laying his hands on him he said, Brother Saul, the Lord Jesus who appeared to you on the road as you came, has sent me that you may receive your sight and be filled with the Holy Spirit." Immediately there fell from his eyes something like scales, and he received his sight at once; and he arose and was baptized.

This happens to most men. Sooner or later, the scales fall off and they can see plainly and think clearer on the things God has been speaking and showing them. The definition of the word blind is simply the inability to see. A person will trip over and run into everything if they cannot see. When God wants you, He will get you! He can change you from your old ways and old habits to serve Him. He can change your entire life! God helps you to drop bad habits and live for Him! You will form good habits like reading the word of God and praying in the spirit. He is the same Jesus that helps people that suffer receive healing power.

God makes Himself manifest by His healing power. The scripture says that nothing is impossible for Him. If you think that a disease is more powerful than the Lord, think again! He cleansed men who had leprosy. They saw it with their own eyes. He restored sight to the blind. The one who was once blind can see things in the physical realm and in the spiritual realm. He even raised Lazarus from the dead. When He raised Lazarus many people saw the power of God right before their very eyes. He restored life into a girl who was dead. When people saw it, you can imagine them giving God the glory and praise!

God has the power to bind anything. To bind means to impose legal or contractual obligation on something. God uses His authority to bind the devil. Listen we can impose authority over attacks in our lives. Another definition is to tie or fasten something. When we speak authority in Jesus name, we tie up the demons. We have the authority to put them in subjection under our feet because of the power of God.

CHAPTER 46
JESUS CALLED YOU!

2 PETER 1:10: Therefore, brethren, be even more diligent to make your call and election sure, for if you do these things you will never stumble; for so an entrance will be supplied to you abundantly into the everlasting kingdom of our Lord and Savior Jesus Christ.

Peter wanted to let people know that their salvation is not based on a good life. He also wanted them to avoid becoming complacent in the ministry and to reject false doctrine. Peter is saying, receive and accept the doctrine of Jesus Christ, our Lord and Redeemer.

An entrance will be supplied for those who hold on to their calling and election. Child of God, keep standing on the word of God. He will never let you go. You can count on Jesus! Your mission is to be ministered to by the Holy Spirit. Your calling is for the Holy Spirit to protect. You have to use your mouth and tongue and speak things into existence by the power of the word. That is why God put the Holy Spirit here. He is your guide and protector. He helps you speak the word with power, authority and boldness. God is still the Most High God and is able to do what He has already predestined for your life.

CHAPTER 47
HE IS RISEN!

MARK 16:1-6: Now when the Sabbath was past, Mary Magdalene, Mary the mother of James, and Salome bought spices, that they might come and anoint Him. Very early in the morning, on the first day of the week, they came to the tomb when the sun had risen. And they said among themselves, "Who will roll away the stone from the door of the tomb for us?" But when they looked up, they saw that the stone had been rolled away for it was very large. And entering the tomb, they saw a young man clothed in a long white robe sitting on the right side; and they were alarmed. But he said to them, "Do not be alarmed. You seek Jesus of Nazareth, who was crucified. He is risen! He is not here. See the place where they laid Him. But go, tell His disciples and Peter that He is going before you into Galilee; there you will see Him, as He said to you.

It is true! He is risen from the dead. The grave could not hold Him because it was all in God's plan. He defeated death. Death holds no victory. Jesus rose from the dead and departed out of the grave with all power in His hand. There is no event in the world that can match what Jesus did. His clothing (veil) remained in the tomb so that witnesses could see it and know that He left the grave. So many people will still miss it. Nothing could keep him in the grave. His clothes were evidence that the power of God had resurrected Him. Jesus to prove that He was God.

CHAPTER 48
LET YOUR REQUEST BE KNOWN

PHIL 4:6-11: Be anxious for nothing, but in everything by prayer and supplication, with thanksgiving, let your requests be made known to God; and the peace of God, which surpasses all understanding, will guard your hearts and minds through Christ Jesus. Finally, brethren, whatever things are true, whatever things are noble, whatever things are just, whatever things are pure, whatever things are lovely, whatever things are of good report, if there is any virtue and if there is anything praiseworthy meditate on these things. The things, which you learned and received and heard and saw in me, these do, and the God of peace will be with you. But I rejoiced in the Lord greatly that now at last your care for me has flourished again; though you surely did care, but you lacked opportunity. Not that I speak in regard to need, for I have learned in whatever state I am, to be content:

God does not want us worrying about anything! When you focus on God, worry goes away. But you need to trust Him for that worry spirit to leave. As you meditate on God even more troubles will leave. The thought of God runs off demons. The thought of God's power brings healing and miracles. Your faith can be activated when your mind is stayed on Him.

The Apostle Paul speaks that he was content in whatever state. Of course that state is the mind of Christ. He was fully aware that Christ Jesus, the same one who delivered Him from his evil ways, would take care all of his needs. If your life has peace and you know that God has filled you with the Holy Spirit then you are aware and fully conscience of the fact that He is.

CHAPTER 49
MAN'S LOVE FOR GOD!

MATTHEW 22:36 Teacher, which is the great commandment in the law? Jesus said to him, you shall love the Lord your God with all your heart, with all your soul, and with all your mind. This is the first and great commandment.

When you show Jesus that you want to walk in obedience to His commands, love surfaces in your heart. God wants man to love Him with his entire being. Open your heart to Jesus and let Him in. Allow your emotions and will to be focused on God's word and service. Put your mind on Him and take it off of ungodly things. Read Galatians 5:16-19. But rather be fruitful in the love of God Galatians 5:22-25. God desires to be first in your life. You will know if you are putting Him first. You will receive blessings above the norm. If you put Him last, you block your blessings and allow the enemy to come in. Start loving God more. The Apostle Paul demonstrated His love by serving God as He preached the gospel. He also wrote two-thirds of the Bible. His love and passion for our Lord Jesus was demonstrated. What can you do to demonstrate your love for Jesus Christ? Surely some people can preach the gospel. But use your spiritual gifts to show love as well. Show love while using your spiritual gifts. Remember to love the Lord with all your heart and love your neighbor as well.

CHAPTER 50
TAME THAT TONGUE!

James 3:8-10 But no man can tame the tongue. It is an unruly evil, full of deadly poison. With it we bless our God and Father, and with it we curse men. Who have been made in the similitude of God. Out of the same mouth proceed blessings and cursing. My brethren these things ought not be so.

Have you ever been around someone that can talk until the lights go off? Do you know someone that really talks too much? I mean it in good spirits. Some people can go on and on to impress others and really think nothing of it. Some people are just social in that way.

The tongue is powerful anyway you look at it. God spoke creation into existence and He made things pleasing in His sight. God's words made Heaven and earth come into being. God spoke and life began. Adam was formed, and then Eve came to life from man. Everything that came out of His mouth was pleasing to Him and for His glorious purpose. God revealed His identity to us through His work of salvation and the words He spoke. We were made to speak blessings and not curses. He gave us these tongues for the proper use of worshiping Him, communicating, and proclaiming blessings on other people lives.

Don't poison anyone with your tongue. If you use the tongue properly, blessings can rain down on you and those around you. The tongue is an instrument to be used for God's glory and edification. The tongue is powerful. It can carry the word of God which is more powerful than a two-edged sword, that pierces and divides the soul and spirit. The word gives life to us. God wants us to stop cursing people with the tongue but rather call out blessings in somebody's life. Proverbs 18:21 tells us that there is life and death in the tongue. The Holy Spirit will lead you to speak life and not death. We must speak life over our children and entire household Speak prosperity and overflowing blessings in the lives of your family and friends. You can do it. Just stop what you are doing now and speak blessings.

CHAPTER 51
EXPECT JESUS TO RETURN

I COR 15:52: In a moment, in the twinkling of an eye, at the last trumpet. For the trumpet will sound, and the dead will be raised incorruptible, and we shall be changed.

Just think, one blink or twinkle of the eye and the entire world could be changed right before us. God is the one who holds all power in His hand. He can do anything. Jesus could return before you can blink an eye. One blink and things could change in your life forever. He could return and pull you up in the air.

Anything can happen. No one knows the time, day nor the hour when Jesus will return, according to the Bible. If you are not careful you could be left behind if you are not born again. John 3:3 says you must be born again. Don't miss out. You will go to hell if you do not accept Jesus as Lord and Savior. You can be here one day and gone the next day. Have you ever had something in your life that affected you so quickly that you did not see it coming? On the other hand, there are things that happen that you expect to happen. You trust that they will happen. For example, you trust that your heart will beat. This is important because there are people who do not understand that their heart is beating because God allows it to beat. If He took it away, you would suffer.

CHAPTER 52
GOD'S GOODNESS

EXODUS 33:18-20: And he said, please show me your glory. Then He said I will make all my goodness pass before you, and I will proclaim the name of the Lord before you. I will be gracious to whom I will be gracious, I will have compassion on whom I will have compassion. But He said, you cannot see my face; for no man shall see me, and live.

This is one of those manifested glory moments that fills the heart with praise, and unspeakable and joy in the Lord. I must admit that I just held back tears to the best of my ability because of what this scripture just said. Moses was the only man to see this manifested glory of God. We are talking about the same God who spoke the universe into existence. Somehow the God of the universe walked in His own manifested glory to reveal to Moses that He is God. He did not have to do it. He did it because of His love and His plan and purpose for Israel. Then there has to be another reason. He wanted to build up His man Moses to show that He is Moses's God. We must always be tied to God.

CHAPTER 53
THE MAN THAT ABIDES IN CHRIST

JOHN 15:7: "If you abide in me, and my words abide in you, you will ask what you desire, and it shall be done for you.

The word abide means simply to remain in Him. Once you become born again in His kingdom, you are in Jesus Christ. Your life is different. In the armed forces, after weeks of intense boot camp, you are officially a soldier. You remain in the Armed Forces as a career soldier. It is better to remain in Him so that the promises He made will really impact your life. Before a skeptic can be transformed into a believer, someone must be able to convince the skeptic that Jesus and God are real, the resurrection did happen, and that Jesus was born of a virgin. The skeptic should be convinced of the cross and the power of forgiveness through the blood of Jesus as the center focus.

You can witness if you remain in Him. Remaining in Him is like a marriage. Once you marry a wife, she expects for you to perform as a husband and never leave her. In Christ, you take on the form of a holy man. Some people have bad habits that they can't seem to break. Some have alcohol or drug issues that they have difficulty breaking. These habits destroy life. It is because they have remained in that habit for so long; reaping the pleasure and damages of that habit.

God wants the opposite for you. You are to abide in Him to reap blessings. When you abide you sow something. Sow your time and service in Christ to reap the benefits of blessings. God knows if you are abiding in Him when you call out blessings. He wants you to call out what you desire so that you can receive it by His power! Not my power or yours, but the power of the Holy Ghost. The Man that abides in Jesus is tougher than 007, Batman, Superman and all of them put together. You see you have power now to tell demons to flee in Jesus name!

CHAPTER 54
WITNESSES OF LIFE

1 CORINTHIANS 15:3-6: For I delivered to you first of all that which I also received: That Christ died for our sins according to the scripture, and that He was buried and that He rose again on the third day according to the scripture, and that He was seen by Cephas, then by the twelve. After that He was seen by five hundred brethren at once, of whom the greater part remain to the present, but some have fallen asleep.

Are you a witness? There were many people who saw Jesus after He rose from the dead. On the third day, He rose from the dead with all power in His hand. God meant for His men to witness Jesus's resurrection. God wanted men to take the lead in witnessing on this earth to people and showing the love of God. Twelve disciples saw Jesus. Five hundred people saw Him after He got up from the grave. Death has no more stings. God declared that Jesus took the sting of death, meaning death can't hold us hostage in the grave. Death does not have authority over us. Jesus has all authority. Because Jesus rose from the grave, we will rise up at the last trumpet according to 1 Thessalonians 4:16.

Sometime in life, you should fulfill your purpose as a witness for Jesus Christ. If you know your purpose, you can make a difference. Tell at least 500 people that He has risen from the dead. Jesus knew His purpose. Tell at least 600 people at your school and in your neighborhood that God has blessed your life because he rose from the dead. Tell 10,000 people that God will pour out more blessings in their life than they can receive. He is the God of the overflow! Tell them we will reign with Him forever. Tell them that God is your redeemer and His blood covers your sin. Tell everybody in the world that Jesus is alive right now and at the right hand of His father in heaven. Give Him Glory and praise and thanksgiving in the house!

CHAPTER 55
CRUCIFIED WITH CHRIST

ROMANS 6:6: knowing this, that our old man was crucified with Him, that the body of sin might be done away with, that we should no longer be slaves of sin.

We must know that all our sin was taken away in the death of Jesus on the cross. The crucifixion was one of the worst forms of execution. Jesus was crucified for us. He hung on the cross, which caused suffocation. He was nailed to it the cross. He had thorns put on his head.

We are asked to crucify our flesh so that we can walk in the Spirit. We are not strong enough to walk alone. The fallen man needs the Holy Spirit to walk with him. To be crucified with Jesus means to put off the old you and clothe yourself in righteousness. To be crucified means to become a living sacrifice. In some cases, we are persecuted, hated, locked up, thrown in prison, and even left for dead. You have to be reminded that you are a new creature in Christ; the old one has passed away.

The power of the cross is what you need to think on the rest of your life. You need to see Jesus hanging on that cross and understand the condition of His body. The power of the cross made us free men. The cross that Jesus was on restored relationships, removed sin, broke the power of the devil and his demons. The cross destroyed the influence and power of sin. Jesus took away the slaves' mentality. The attacks of the enemy are blocked.

Jesus rescued me from cocaine, ecstasy, marijuana and a host of other drugs. The Apostle Paul said in Philippians 3:10 "that I may know Him and the power of His resurrection, and the fellowship of His sufferings, being conformed to His death," You should get your sights set on Him and know Him. He is the only true and wise God. He is the redeemer of my soul and yours.

CHAPTER 56
NEW LIFE!

ROMANS 6:4: Therefore we were buried with Him through baptism into death, that just as Christ was raised from the dead by the glory of the Father, even so we should also walk in the newness of life.

Do you know if your husband and sons are baptized? It is time for a new life experience. This is a time for the wife to address her husband. It's time for man to be confronted by God. Matthew 28 is a command that Jesus gave His disciples to get people baptized in the name of the Father, Son and Holy Ghost. You can have a new life in Christ Jesus any time you want it. It is available 24-7. Jesus make us a part of his burial and resurrection because we believe in Him. The cross, burial and resurrection of Jesus is the foundation of Christianity. It is the core of the Bible with Jesus reflected in both the Old and New Testaments. It's time to die to old things and come alive in Jesus Christ.

The good thing about this is that you do not have to beg for it. Just surrender. You do not have to purchase it because Jesus already paid the price on the cross. God already knows your heart's desire. Start trusting God today. He will bless you. You need to repent of your sin and ask Jesus to come into your heart right now. Baptism symbolizes our action and agreement in Christ's resurrection. It is a testament to our faith in the death, burial, and resurrection of our Lord, Jesus Christ. The baptism is symbolic to our walk in the newness of Jesus Christ. Start claiming that you are a new man! Walk in a new life and let somebody see the Christ in you.

CHAPTER 57
A FATHER'S LOVE FOR SONS

LUKE 15:15-23: Then he went and joined himself to a citizen of that country, and he sent him into his fields to feed swine. And he would gladly have filled his stomach with the pods that the swine ate, and no one gave him anything. "But when he came to himself, he said, 'How many of my father's hired servants have bread enough and to spare, and I perish with hunger! I will arise and go to my father, and will say to him, "Father, I have sinned against heaven and before you, and I am no longer worthy to be called your son. Make me like one of your hired servants."' "And he arose and came to his father. But when he was still a great way off, his father saw him and had compassion, and ran and fell on his neck and kissed him. And the son said to him, 'Father, I have sinned against heaven and in your sight, and am no longer worthy to be called your son.' "But the father said to his servants, 'Bring out the best robe and put it on him, and put a ring on his hand and sandals on his feet. And bring the fatted calf here and kill it, and let us eat and be merry.

Every man dreams of being a father. His first thought when he meets the woman of his dream is that she will give him a son. It is not that a daughter is lesser. It is just that men expect to see their sons take over where they leave off in business. There is also that inner man connection to God. We were made to connect to God and be blessed! A man wants a miniature picture of himself. He wants to see what His seed has produced. God has built that in him.

Most sons are loaded with ambition. Many have some type of training, and the desire to achieve. When they cry for help, it is a different sound. God makes known the blessing. Instinctively, most men are aware of the need to step in and nurture his son in particularly in Jesus Christ. As men, we need to step in and step up.

I've discovered that my son is hearing, but not always listening. In other words, nothing effective is happening so you have to take sons back to the word of God. Nothing gets away from the Jesus when He is speaking. Give them to God!

CHAPTER 58
GOD-GIVEN AUTHORITY TO MAN

Genesis 2:18-24 The Lord God said, "It is not good for the man to be alone. I will make a helper suitable for him. "Now the Lord God had formed out of the ground all the wild animals and all the birds in the sky. He brought them to the man to see what he would name them; and whatever the man called each living creature, that was its name. So the man gave names to all the livestock, the birds in the sky and all the wild animals. But for Adam no suitable helper was found. So the Lord God caused the man to fall into a deep sleep; and while he was sleeping, he took one of the man's ribs and then closed up the place with flesh. Then the Lord God made a woman from the rib he had taken out of the man, and he brought her to the man. The man said, "This is now bone of my bones and flesh of my flesh; she shall be called 'woman,' for she was taken out of man." That is why a man leaves his father and mother and is united to his wife, and they become one flesh.

God made sure He fulfilled man's every need. Then God gave Adam power over all creation. God gave man power to name every animal. Since God gave man power then, he still has that power.

God may have seen loneliness in man's heart so he took a rib from man and made him a woman to help him. God purposely married them. The Bible is clear that God brought the woman to Adam as a bride. Your wife is ordained to be your bride for a lifetime. Pornography and lust are not substitutes for love and sex. Your wife according to Ephesians 5 must be submissive to you. Everything you need in sex comes from your wife. She is not to withhold anything that God made to support her husband. Likewise the man is to love her as Christ loved the Church. He must be a God-fearing man, living in obedience in order to make the marriage work!

The Bible is very clear that Adam spoke into the life of his wife his expectations. Adam said, "This is bone of my bones and flesh of my flesh; which can also be taken as she is everything to me as God fulfilled my needs.

She is to be respectful, honorable and an obedient wife as the helper God made her to be. She is not to look upon another man and lust or have sexual intimacy with any other. She is to be only submissive to her own husband.

CHAPTER 59
WALKING IN FAVOR

EPHESIANS 2:8 For by grace are ye saved through faith; and that not of yourselves: it is the gift of God: Not of works, lest any man should boast.

Because of grace, you walk in the blessed life! You are automatically walking in favor as a believer! God is looking for fathers to walk in grace. Grace is unmerited favor. We did not earn it. God gave it because of His love for humanity. If you walk in grace, you will walk in obedience. Then God can use you in His Kingdom as a Kingdom Man. God has supplied grace in the life of every person so there is no excuse for a man. He must turn his life over to God by accepting Jesus into his heart. The same applies to women.

Athletes who participate in the Olympics are good examples of people who want to win a medal and be on top of the world. People risk it all for the opportunity to tell their story. It would be better to tell everyone you get a chance to about Jesus. Take a risk to lead one or a thousand to salvation. It is free for all people.

Lead them in this prayer, "Lord forgive me of my sin, Please come into my heart. I believe that you are the Son of God. I believe that you died on the cross for my sin and the Father raised you from the dead on the third day that I might live eternally." Walk in favor from now on. Stay positive and walk in God's favor. It's free, so tell your neighbors and every United States Army, Marine, and Air Force soldier about God's grace and favor given to us. Go out and witness today. Lift up the name that is above every name, Jesus Christ! Give Him glory!

CHAPTER 60
THE ORIGINAL MAN ADVANCED

Genesis 2:7-8 the Lord God formed man of the dust of the ground, and breathed into his nostrils the breath of life; and man became a living soul. And the Lord God planted a garden eastward in Eden; and there he put the man whom he had formed.

Adam was the first man formed by God. It is safe to say that we received our roots from Adam through God's power. The word formed means to make or fashion into a certain shape. The Greek word for formed is plastòs, which means to properly shape, to mold and to makeup. The word form also sends the meaning or idea of using clay to mold or create something unique.

If you ever have an identity crisis, look back and remember where you came from. Consider from where did your ancestors come. You did not evolve from an animal! You came from previous generations of ancestors which came from God. According to Genesis 2, God formed man from the ground, the dirt. The importance of this passage is this: You were made in the image of God and filled with power to follow God all of your life. Why? You were made this way to fulfill your purpose by serving God. God built and designed each man with the power to love. You are a special blueprint made from God. God also gave man dominion and authority over everything that He created.

The original idea is for man to have peace. He was to be a man of honor and life worshiping God only. He was to never waiver and make excuses when it came to serving God. However the original man needed Jesus to redeem him with His blood because he stepped out of obedience. The main idea is that every man returns to God. God also wants you to bring your sons and daughters back to Him as well, so He can bless them. Don't reject the grace! Don't reject His proven love. Don't reject God cleaning you up and restoring your life!

Break all your bad habits and serve the living God. As a man of God, you can put down the drugs, stop the abuse of your wife and children, you can let go of past pain. You can get over those scars that others left on you. You are God's man now! You are an advanced man of God because you are in Jesus Christ. His spirit dwells inside of your heart. Your vessel belongs to Him! You are to live a surrendered life in Jesus Christ. God wants you to live in paradise, in this world and the world to come!

CHAPTER 61
THE COVENANT MAN

Genesis 17:5-7 Neither shall thy name any more be called Abram, but thy name shall be Abraham; for a father of many nations have I made thee. And I will make thee exceeding fruitful, and I will make nations of thee, and kings shall come out of thee. And I will establish my covenant between me and thee and thy seed after thee in their generations for an everlasting covenant, to be a God unto thee, and to thy seed after thee.

What is a covenant? A covenant is an agreement. It is a legal contract; a promise. Abraham is known as the father of many nations because God blessed him and made a covenant with him. His name was Abram in the beginning and it was changed by God to Abraham to signify that he had a covenant with God.

Abraham is well known for moving away from his family when God told him to move. Abraham was a covenant-keeping man. The scripture points us to the Abrahamic Covenant. God made a covenant with Himself in **Genesis 17:1-16, Genesis 17:5-6, Genesis 2:9-11, and Genesis 3:14, Galatians 3:26-29.** Abram received specific instructions from God to lay out a sacrifice (his son) so that God could show up.

We now have the new covenant by Jesus Christ. Hebrews 9, 10; 1 Corinthians 11:24-34. Nothing is greater than the new covenant. God allowed for the new covenant through Jesus Christ, His Son, because no other sacrifice could suffice. We deserved the wrath of God as our penalty for sin. But Jesus took our place. We are walking in Jesus' covenant. He is the absolute only true and wise Savior. The Lord our God is merciful forever and ever. God is looking for a covenant man and people that will agree with and serve Him. God is looking for a covenant man to release blessings in His name! He loves to see the covenant man walking in obedience. A covenant man is an obedient man of God. God can deliver you from all hurt, trouble and pain. He is able to bring you from hardship to blessing. Once you have been bought with a price, God is able to turn your life around.

He is my redeemer. He lives for me! I know He lives. He is the one who blesses my life. He is the covenant keeper and He never breaks a promise. You might want to study Noah, King David, Abraham, Moses and Joseph. They all had a covenant with God.

CHAPTER 62
MOSES, THE DELIVERER

All types of spirits were imbedded in Pharaoh's camp. Pharaoh indicated that he really did not care about the life of people. God wants us to know that He will intervene on behalf of his people whenever He is needed. The Bible tells us that God heard the cry of His people by the affliction of those task masters. They were constantly beating and tormenting God's people. When God hears your cry, He will step in and rescue you. We all are looking for deliverance in some form or fashion.

Moses walked in power to deliver God's people and give them victory. God expects all of His saints to operate in this same power. When the time came, Moses was chosen to be a deliverer to the Hebrew people in the Old Testament. He was used by God to deliver thousands of people out of bondage. Regardless of Pharaoh's attitude and resistance to Moses, God's power always makes the difference. God used Moses to accomplish his will. Moses could not stop approaching Pharaoh just because he wanted him to stop. God sent plagues to Egypt to prove that He was serious about Moses visitations and his people coming out of slavery. God used Moses to hold up his staff by faith and the red sea opened. His people moved to the other side and Pharaoh's army drowned.

You may have never been used by God. But God wants to use you, now. Do not wait another day, turn your life over to Jesus and be born again and used in God's Kingdom. You are the kind of person God is looking to use in His army. Be one of God's deliverers in Jesus name!

CHAPTER 63
LORD, BLESS ME!

Genesis 32:28 And he said, Thy name shall be called no more Jacob, but Israel: for as a prince hast thou power with God and with men, and hast prevailed.

God wants a man that will seek to get blessed! Jacob is one of God's men of honor. God saw the resilience in Jacob's life when he wrestled all night long with an angel. He made the statement that most of us remember in Genesis 32. "I will not let go until you bless me. " It's ironic that he asked God to bless him after he had also stolen his brother Esau's blessing, the birthright. Jacob was one bold brother to make such a statement to God. Of course, he had his mother on his side. Jacob was smart enough to know that whatever He needed from God, he could ask..

Jacob was the younger of the twins. He was known as a trickster, surplanter and deceiver. He earned this title, not only from deceiving his father to get Esau's blessings, he also grabbed hold of his brother's heel as they were being delivered in birth from his mother's womb. Can you imagine having that attitude at birth, desiring to be first? God is looking for that kind of attitude and boldness in His people. God is looking for his people to have a desire to be blessed of the Lord. He is also looking for someone who will put up a fight for His blessings.

God is looking for men who will put forth the effort of wrestling all night until they get the blessing they want and what God will grant them. It's amazing that God would take the time out to measure a man's boldness, tenacity and zeal to get a blessing. He wants you to obey his directions, break the bad habits you have, and learn to love others that you have neglected. God wants you to worship Him in spirit and truth.

You need to grab hold to God the best way you know how. He can break us from our old ways to make us into a new man! It will require that we read the word man of God and pray. As a result of wrestling to the break of dawn, Jacob's identity was changed to Israel. This reflects God's chosen people. God allowed Jacob to go through this struggle. Jacob's thigh was dislocated. God wanted to see if He would still hold on to get the blessing. If he could make it through the struggle (by wrestling with God's angel), he could be a leader in God's army and his household; and walk as a blessed man.

His limp represented that He was a changed man and anointed because he had been with God. Because Jacob did not let go, his seed was blessed and multiplied. His life was blessed and anointed. He had 12 sons. Men want sons to receive their inheritance and name. Jacob was responsible for the seed of the 12 tribes of Israel. He asked God to bless Him! God is looking for more men to bless. He has more blessings to give than man can imagine. God operates in the overflow of blessings. Jacob's sons were to multiply and be a blessing in God's Kingdom among His chosen people. God has a plan for you man of God! Ask for the blessing and walk in it (Genesis 32:26-28).

CHAPTER 64
WHEN DREAMS COME TRUE

Genesis 37:1-50

Joseph is another one of God's leading men. Joseph had the right attitude toward God. Joseph stands out from the very beginning to the end of his story as a blessed man. I believe it was because Jacob asked God for blessings. All of those blessings transferred to his sons and Joseph was one of Jacob's sons, known as the favorite and younger of the brothers. Jacob even gave Joseph a coat of royalty (coat of many colors). Joseph told his family of a dream he had and that they would all someday bow before him. It is important that you know that God is looking for this kind of heart in a man. Believe in the dreams that God gives you. He is constructing and shaping something in your life just as He was doing in Joseph's life. Some dreams are blessings. On the other hand, some dreams can be nightmares.

Joseph's dreams were a set up for blessing His family and Egypt. After he told his family the dream and how they would bow before him, they threw him in a pit and left him for dead. They even reported it back to Jacob.

Joseph went from the pit to being sold into slavery. He ended up working for Potiphar and because of his right spirit and obedience to God; he impressed everyone he came into contact with, even after they drew him in prison.

Pharaoh was so impressed with Joseph after he interpreted his dreams that God touched his heart. He declared Joseph second in command of all of Egypt. Joseph's brothers did bow before him. God set it up to show the world that Joseph was a blessed man of God. Joseph was a strategist with a godly wisdom. He would arrange harvest to be stored and it would last through the worst storms. If he hadn't, it could have easily left Egypt in drought and famine. It was Joseph who saved Egypt and his family from destruction.

God wants every man to have a Joseph spirit. You can save your house from destruction and ask God to bless it. Dreams do come true when God is in them! God ordains the blessing over His people. Joseph's dreams were filled with the abundance of blessings. God can do the same for you and me in our dreams. Spend time with God and walk in blessings.

CHAPTER 65
JOB, A FAITHFUL MAN OF GOD

Job 1:8 And the Lord said unto Satan, Hast thou considered my servant Job, that there is none like him in the earth, a perfect and an upright man, one that feareth God, and escheweth evil?

We all experience something in life. But God wants us to know that we may also have experiences similar to Job. The devil had to get permission to touch Job's life. He was not authorized to kill him. God set out to show the devil that he has no grip! You can't keep God's people down! Through the life of Job, God shows man that life can get bad, but it can be turned around. Job experienced it. The devil was involved in destroying his family, but we couldn't touch Job. God will put you to the test in one way or another. You are a man and a man has to stand for God or stand for nothing. Job is the example of a man who trusted God through the hardest, roughest, hurtful, and the most devastating of times. There are several major points in Job's story. One point is to demonstrate Job's trust of God no matter what happened. Another point to consider is to never get out of the will of God. Job made the most profound statement when he said, **I know that my redeemer liveth.** Those are the words of a true man of God. **Though he slay me, yet will I trust in Him: I will maintain my own ways before him. Job13:15.**

In my sermon on Sunday, I was reminded by the Holy Spirit to tell the people that God has a way of protecting and blessing you when it seems like the world has fallen on your shoulders. Satan destroyed Job's family. But Job still did not leave God. Because of his trust and faithfulness in the Lord, he received double for the trouble the enemy caused. The enemy had to get permission from God to do the damage he did. But God told him that he could touch

Job's life but not kill him. Has your life been touched by the enemy?

CHAPTER 66
LISTENING TO GOD'S VOICE
A MAN OF GRACE

Genesis 6:8 But Noah found grace in the eyes of the Lord.

Noah was truly a man of God. One of the single major characteristics about Noah was that His listened to the voice of God. It is rare that people listen to the voice of God. Noah not only listened to the voice of God, he heeded to the instructions given to him to construct an ark for the saving and regeneration of life. Because of Noah's actions, God said that Noah found grace in the eyes of God. What a powerful statement! This means obviously that God was pleased with Noah and blessed Him. Imagine how many people it really should have taken to construct that ark. Noah devoted his time and energy to constructing this ark for God's use.

Obedience to God's voice is the lesson the Lord is showing us. Being faithful to God helps you walk and act on behalf of God. When will you be obedient to the voice of God in your church, at home or even at your job? God is asking you to be faithful and obedient when He calls on you for a mission. He's instructing you to do something. He has purpose for you to make a difference in somebody's life. But are you listening? Listen to God today and get blessed!

CHAPTER 67
SAMSON, THE MAN JUDGES 16

Judges 16:3-4 And Samson lay till midnight, and arose at midnight, and took the doors of the gate of the city, and the two posts, and went away with them, bar and all, and put them upon his shoulders, and carried them up to the top of an hill that is before Hebron. And it came to pass afterward, that he loved a woman in the valley of Sorek, whose name was Delilah.

Most people have heard about Samson in the Bible. Perhaps, the first thought for most people is his amazing strength that he used to defeat all his enemies. He was a man that God specifically equipped to have amazing strength to reflect the Lord was with him. Samson was a Nazerite. He was to stay away from drinks and sin. Samson received his strength from God. Strength is what we all need. It is hard to live without it. It is remarkable that we get renewed strength every day of our lives and it comes directly from God. We need to be thankful for that.

Samson had several situations facing him. One immediate issue was his love for a woman named Delilah. When Samson met Delilah, his life was altered. He was warned by His mother. This is when hell broke loose in his life. A man can handle just about anything, but when an attack comes at his heart from a woman he loves, life becomes hellish. His love for her was his weakness and caused him to turn from God. The woman and the enemy made him lose his strength for a moment and put his eyes out. His other problem was the Philistine army. The Philistines represent the enemy. The enemy is chasing us all of the time to take us down.

The Philistines used Samson's woman to betray him. He gave in to her seductive spirit and told her his secret: his strength was in his hair. She told the Philistines and they took advantage of his weakness and blinded him. He would later get revenge when he returned to God. Only when he returned to God was he able to defeat his enemies. God tells us all, that when you turn to me you will gain strength to overcome your enemies. The main points of this story are that we must know to whom we really belong and we must be obedient to the instructions given by God.

Man, don't try to live this course of life on your own good merits, and personal wisdom. You need Godly wisdom and the Holy Spirit's guidance (John 16).

CHAPTER 68
LOVE IS THE GREATEST

I CORINTHIANS 13:13 And now abideth faith, hope, charity, these three; but the greatest of these is charity.

Love extends beyond all things! It is the priority in life and in every family. When we think of love, we often think of a romance story. For some people love and romance stories take their breath away. One movie called "Notebook" displayed the love of a married couple. Some people are looking for the "Cinderella story" type of love. Some like to think of Romeo and Juliet love, where a man pours out his heart for a beautiful woman. More importantly people want real love even after the fairytale. No one can truly live without love. However there is no love greater than the love of God (**John 3:16**).

Jesus displayed the ultimate love on the cross. Nothing compares to His love. God's love is what sustains us daily. We look for love from our parents. Husbands and wives look for love from each other. Children look for love from parents. Love is essential.

The Bible speaks of agape love, which is unconditional love. Unconditional love is the love God gives to us. People offer phileo love. This kind of love is conditional. People want something for love. Most people do not experience agape love in marriages. The enemy attacks wives to make them want something in exchange for their love which is not according to the word of God. Every couple needs to read Ephesians 5, Peter 3 and 1 Corinthian 7. This applies to keeping intimate love alive and under God's plan for marriages.

The most important thing is that you understand that it was God's love that took Jesus to Calvary. His love took the sentence for every single person in the world. Do you love God? How do you show it to Him? Will you give Jesus your heart since you know that He only wants to love you and bless you? **ROMANS 8:38-41**

CHAPTER 69
SEED SOWERS

Be a person who sows into the Kingdom of God.

Mark 4:26-29 And he said, "The kingdom of God is as if a man should scatter seed on the ground. He sleeps and rises night and day, and the seed sprouts and grows; he knows not how. The earth produces by itself, first the blade, then the ear, then the full grain in the ear. But when the grain is ripe, at once he puts in the sickle, because the harvest has come."

Luke 8:11 Now the parable is this: The seed is the word of God.

Genesis 8:22 While the earth remaineth, seedtime and harvest, and cold and heat, and summer and winter, and day and night shall not cease.

2 Corinthians 9:10-11 Now he that ministereth seed to the sower both minister bread for your food, and multiply your seed sown, and increase the fruits of your righteousness;) Being enriched in every thing to all bountifulness, which causeth through us thanksgiving to God.

Luke 8:15 But that on the good ground are they, which in an honest and good heart, having heard the word, keep it, and bring forth fruit with patience.

Luke 8:5 A sower went out to sow his seed: and as he sowed, some fell by the way side; and it was trodden down, and the fowls of the air devoured it.

Genesis 26:12-13 Then Isaac sowed in that land, and received in the same year an hundredfold: and the Lord blessed him.

And the man waxed great, and went forward, and grew until he became very great:

Galatians 6:8 For he that soweth to his flesh shall of the flesh reap corruption; but he that soweth to the Spirit shall of the Spirit reap life everlasting.

God wants His people to get in the habit of sowing seed so you can please Him. A giving heart to God reflects obedience and unselfish spirit. God's word teaches us to sow for Kingdom purposes. We get blessed when we sow in His kingdom. Our sowing also reflects where are hearts are. He does not want our money, financial gains, profits, assets or any things of value to take first place and control the heart. He wants us to be cheerful in financial sowing as well as sowing the word of God. Try doing both and see how your heart feels in the Lord, Jesus Christ. You were put on this earth for a purpose. Sow the word of God and sow your first fruits unto the Lord. Live the blessed life as a sower in God's Kingdom.

CHAPTER 70
DWELL WITH MY FATHER!

Revelation 21:1-7 And I saw a new heaven and a new earth: for the first heaven and the first earth were passed away; and there was no more sea. And I John saw the holy city, New Jerusalem, coming down from God out of heaven, prepared as a bride adorned for her husband. And I heard a great voice out of heaven saying, Behold, the tabernacle of God is with men, and he will dwell with them, and they shall be his people, and God himself shall be with them, and be their God. And God shall wipe away all tears from their eyes; and there shall be no more death, neither sorrow, nor crying, neither shall there be any more pain: for the former things are passed away. And he that sat upon the throne said, Behold, I make all things new. And he said unto me, Write: for these words are true and faithful. And he said unto me, It is done. I am Alpha and Omega, the beginning and the end. I will give unto him that is athirst of the fountain of the water of life freely. He that overcometh shall inherit all things; and I will be his God, and he shall be my son.

Imagine what life will be like with God. He makes everything so comforting. The thought of being with my Father in heaven makes it alright! I know without a shadow of doubt that my Redeemer lives and I will be with Him, one day. Meanwhile, I will serve Him to the end of my time, according to His will.

God is looking for men with an attitude to serve and know Him. We will dwell with our father in heaven here on earth and when the time comes in heaven. We can proclaim to the world that God is the Alpha and Omega, the beginning and end. Find peace in His presence. Find a way out of your circumstances to God. Make Him the ruler of your life. It's time to break away from everything that has you in bondage and ask God to be your God. Dwell with God so He can change your life and identity. Dwell with the Lord because you want to live with Him forever!

Tell a friend that may be in trouble or someone who has lost a loved one that God will comfort them and wipe away tears from their eyes and make them smile again. He will do it because of His great love for all people. Take on the attitude that you can trust God in everything. Get your relationship with Jesus so that you will live and reign with Him forever and ever!

ABOUT THE AUTHOR

Joseph Harris currently lives in Texas. He is retired from the United States Armed Forces. However, he continues to work in support of wounded soldiers returning from war.

He is the Pastor and Founder of Christian Worship Outreach Center
Ministries. His mission is to preach the Gospel of Jesus Christ! His focus
and foundation is the word of God . He is a Kingdom Builder. He delights in introducing others to receive Jesus Christ, as Lord and Savior.

Pastor Harris is a husband and father.   He is also the author of several other books: Fallen Scales, Reverse the Tide, The God Hold on Me,
    Transformation Man, and Rock the Pedestal.

www.ingramcontent.com/pod-product-compliance
Lightning Source LLC
Chambersburg PA
CBHW070459090426
42735CB00012B/2617